KEYBOARD
with GREATER SUCCESS
and SATISFACTION

**by WESLEY SCHAUM
and JOAN CUPP**

SCHAUM PUBLICATIONS
Mequon, Wisconsin 53092

Fifth Printing
© Copyright 1985, 1987, 1991, 1994 and 1998 by Schaum Publications, Inc.
International Copyright Secured
All Rights Reserved
Published by Schaum Publications, Inc.
10235 N. Port Washington Road, Mequon, WI 53092
Printed in United States of America

FOREWORD

The art of teaching is a process of continuing development involving years of study, experience, and hard work. The dedicated teacher never stops searching for ways of self-improvement. This book is for those who want to refine their teaching skills and gain new ideas. The topics range from ethics, philosophy, and psychology to advertising, record keeping, and collecting money. The explanations contain sufficient detail so that even a beginning teacher can benefit. It is hoped that experienced teachers will view the obvious as a refresher and concentrate on those portions of the text that complement their level of expertise.

As you have discovered, private teaching has many advantages. Because you are self-employed, you work just as much as you want and at the times you choose. If you are able to teach in your own home, expenses are easily kept at a minimum. It is one of the few professions, in most areas, that does not require a license or degree. And there really is a *need* for good, conscientious keyboard teachers.

Obviously, it is essential that you enjoy working with people and recognize that each student is an individual personality with different musical goals and limitations in ability. Other necessary attributes of a good teacher are:

1. A true love of music.

2. Abundant patience.

3. A sense of humor and an open mind.

4. Willingness to be part counselor, part psychologist, and part mind-reader.

5. An enthusiastic attitude that is contagious!

We sincerely hope that this book will enhance and give a new perspective to your teaching!

Wesley Schaum and Joan Cupp

CONTENTS

ETHICS, GOALS and PSYCHOLOGY

HOW to ACQUIRE and KEEP STUDENTS

PRACTICAL ASPECTS of TEACHING

RELATIONSHIPS of TEACHER, STUDENT and PARENT

MUSICIANSHIP DEVELOPMENT

CHOOSING TEACHING MATERIALS

LESSON PLANNING

HANDLING SPECIAL SITUATIONS

NEW HORIZONS

46. TEACHING PROGRAMS for EACH LEVEL

That was excellent, Jess.
Now let's unplug it
and try it without the roller.

ETHICS, GOALS, and PSYCHOLOGY

CHAPTER 1

QUALIFICATIONS and ETHICS of TEACHING

No one should attempt teaching without mastering at least Level Six (F or Grade 4) in their own keyboard study. A teacher with this minimum background should not try to teach students beyond Level Four (D or Grade 2½).

Until you are competent with more advanced levels of music, it is better to turn advanced students over to a more experienced teacher than to risk a reputation-in-the-making by attempting to teach beyond your own ability.

Teaching is a *profession,* not just a job. In seeking to fill your schedule, never "put down" another teacher. Always remember, everyone in the music profession has something of value to share, even if their ideas or approach differ from yours. It's easy to be critical but often difficult to do things better yourself.

Teach thoroughly and conscientiously. Seek constantly to improve your keyboard skills and broaden your musical experiences. Growth in your reputation as a teacher will be the result.

Ethically, the obligations of a private teacher include:

1. Between Teacher and Student. You should always try to give each pupil your full attention and best teaching efforts during the lesson time. Although it may sometimes be difficult, try to forget about your family, other cares, and obligations and focus on the needs of the student. The attitude, care, and efforts you show during each lesson are reflected in the attitude and progress of the student. Conscientious teaching nurtures conscientious pupils.

2. Between Teacher and Parents. Parents are entitled to be regularly and candidly informed about their child's progress, be it good, bad, or indifferent. As a teacher you should encourage and maintain communications with parents. Some problems that arise during a lesson, such as disrespect, inattention, or continued lack of practice, require prompt contact with parents. In the long run, your reputation as a teacher depends upon your effectiveness in communicating with parents.

3. Evaluation of Musical Progress. When you first accept a pupil, either a new beginner or a transfer student, you should discuss with parent and child their *purpose and expectations* for music study. Most students take keyboard lessons as a hobby and for various personal and social benefits that are discussed in Chapter 3, "Benefits of Keyboard Study." Occasionally, you encounter parents who have greater ambitions for their child. When this is known in advance, it is best to agree on a reasonable trial period, such as three or four months, for you to evaluate a pupil's musical potential.

How long do you continue teaching a student with obviously little musical ability (even when both student and parents are eager)?

How long do you teach a student who is indifferent and shows minimal progress (even when parents want to continue)?

Answers to these questions depend on the results of a frank discussion with the parents. In some cases, they will ask you to continue teaching because of personal or even therapeutic benefits, even when the musical expectations are slim. Other parents may want to try a different teacher, much as you might go to another physician for a "second opinion." Even though you might lose the student, it is far better to discontinue lessons than to disillusion either child or parents with false hopes. This is very important to your credibility and reputation as a teacher.

Your decision to stop teaching a marginal student, even if parents are willing to have their child continue, will also depend on your answers to these questions:

Do you have a waiting list of other more promising students?

Do you *personally* like working with the student, or is it too much of a bother? Would you rather be doing something else?

Are the parents *really supportive* of their child, or do you get the feeling that you're a high-priced baby sitter?

Always try to remember two things. First, even if a student never attains significant musical skill, study in itself has a good influence. If nothing else, the student will learn something of diligence, responsibility, and study habits along with some understanding of music and a greater appreciation of it. It is surprising what students of limited ability can accomplish if dedicated and motivated with perseverance.

Second, when evaluating a student's musical talent and potential, there is always the possibility of error. Another teacher may view the same student quite differently. The age and maturity of a child, especially age seven and under, will make a great difference. Children vary widely in the age and manner that their musical abilities show up.

4. Respect for Copyright Laws. Original music, lyrics to songs, and musical arrangements are among creative works which are protected by U.S. copyright law. Copyright coverage includes all printed forms, films, and electronic media, including Xerox (and any other method of photocopy), transparencies, filmstrips, slides, cassette recordings, phonograph records, compact disks, video tapes, video disks, and movies.

The law is clear. Those who make unauthorized copies, reproductions, or recordings *for any reason* are subject to penalty. This includes lyrics for song sheets, special arrangements of music, extra copies (for audition, festival, or contest), and custom recordings.

If you want to use copyrighted materials, *always ask permission first!* Allow at least three weeks for a reply. If you're in a hurry, pick up the phone.

For more information, write to: Copyright Office, Library of Congress, Washington, D.C. 20559.

CHAPTER 2

OUTLOOK TOWARD TEACHING

Teaching should not be taken lightly! It is not merely a hobby, something to pass the time, or simply a means of making money. With this profession comes the awesome responsibility of nurturing young people into their teenage years and sometimes beyond. As a conscientious teacher, your influence should extend to students' personal development as well as their music instruction.

The talent needed for success at the keyboard is a blend of many abilities. Obviously, a musical ear, good memory and feeling for rhythm are necessary. Also needed is the coordination of ears, eyes, fingers and muscles. The students you get will have a mixture of such blessings. It will be up to you to help each pupil make the best of his/her natural endowments. The Schaum teaching system enables you to accommodate students of varying abilities.

The primary purpose of the private teacher is to make music and the keyboard an enjoyable and rewarding experience for as many students as possible, regardless of their musical abilities. A slogan, which became part of John W. Schaum's teaching philosophy, applies here. "It's not what the child does for music, but *what music does for the child.*"

Don't spurn students who seem to have little musical talent. It sometimes takes many months for a child to respond to private teaching. If you can make the parents aware of this, your work at the keyboard can be of great emotional and personal benefit to the student, even though the musical results may be very limited.

CHAPTER 3

BENEFITS of KEYBOARD STUDY

Keyboard lessons are *more* than just learning to read music and playing pieces. Here are some of the ways your teaching can be an important influence on the student, both musically and personally.

A. Instills Self-Discipline. Music lessons are probably the very first adventure the young child will experience in realizing that only he/she *alone* can accomplish the results desired. You can help instill a sense of responsibility which carries over into other activities.

B. Increases Concentration Span. Learning to play a keyboard instrument requires strict attention. To effectively keep a steady beat, play the correct notes, pedal properly, and interpret all dynamic marks, the student is forced to continually look ahead one or more measures. Looking around the room or allowing the mind to wander is disastrous. Music demands the ability to concentrate, at first in small segments, then in gradually larger portions of time.

C. Develops Coordination. Music improves coordination between thought and action. It requires mental alertness, accuracy, and good memory. Imagine the thought process required when playing the piano or organ. The eye sees the music and sends a message to the brain, triggering movements of fingers and feet as needed.

D. Provides Emotional Release. Everyone has the basic need to express themselves — young and old. Music is called the universal language because it has no boundaries in expressing all the emotions of life such as joy, sorrow, and excitement. Music helps create an emotional release in both performer and listener.

E. Instills Self-Confidence and Poise. Keyboard playing gives the student a feeling of accomplishment and satisfaction. Social acceptance comes much easier for the child who is willing to share his musical training with an audience.

F. Becomes a Foundation for Other Musical Pursuits. Piano is a basic instrument that serves as a foundation for other musical activities while growing up and also during adulthood. Knowledge of the keyboard is a valuable asset when singing in a school vocal group or church choir. The musicianship learned at the keyboard also is a big help when learning a band or orchestra instrument.

G. Instills a Love and Appreciation of Music. Probably the most lasting value of keyboard study is the love and appreciation of music that is fostered during lessons. The important *roots of good musical taste* are also formed during keyboard study. These are values that *endure throughout adult life.*

H. Therapy for Handicapped and Learning Disabled. Music can be a marvelous tool for helping learning disabled and handicapped students. Although the teaching must be tailored to the individual, and progress is usually quite slow and limited, such students are often very responsive and appreciative.

CHAPTER 4

TEACHING GOALS and CONTINUED EDUCATION

As you have discovered, there are many intangible rewards that come from teaching. Seeing your students grow from those first A-B-C's to playing beautiful pieces, performing for music classes at school, talent shows, or bringing special music to a religious program will all bring great satisfaction to you. You may have some who become able to accompany a choir or school choral group. A few may even aim at a musical career.

A student's response to your playing brings another special kind of joy to both of you. We may forget that our students are constantly looking at us as a model. Beware of complacency! We should frequently evaluate *our own* musical progress and outlook as well as that of our students. Teachers who appear tired, bored, uninspired, or preoccupied with "something more important" are inviting student dropouts!

Obviously, we must regularly devote time to maintaining and improving our own musical skills and knowledge. This requires self-discipline to *make time* for our own daily practice. Even 10 or 15 minutes of concentrated practice each day can do wonders.

As your students progress from book to book and gain in proficiency and confidence, you may experience some feelings of insecurity. For example, every now and then you will have the good fortune to acquire a student who seems to soak up everything you teach, like a sponge. You will need to work a little harder to keep ahead of such a pupil. To be a good teacher involves a constant process of learning from which one never graduates. Let's examine some of the possible ways to further your own education.

1. Teachers often take lessons themselves, either from another private teacher who is more advanced, or by enrolling at a nearby college or conservatory. These lessons can be fun, if only to refresh what you had learned some time ago — or can be a time of learning completely new techniques, repertoire, and information that can be passed on to your students.

2. There are many seminars for keyboard teachers offered throughout the country during the year. Many are short, half-day sessions sponsored by local musical dealers and offered without charge. Others are held at a college campus or conservatory. The length varies from one to four days, usually with a registration fee.

3. If you want to augment or review your knowledge of music theory, harmony, pedagogy, history, or literature, a college or conservatory will have classes that you can take as an "auditor." The fee is less, and although you get no credit toward a degree, you are not obligated to do all the homework assignments. You may also find a private teacher who is equipped to offer help in theory and harmony.

4. Local, county, or regional music teacher organizations offer opportunities for membership. They are variously called music clubs, teacher guilds, or associations. A group of *private* music teachers would probably be of most benefit to you. Other organizations are primarily for public school music teachers. The private teacher groups may be exclusively for keyboard or may offer membership to teachers of any instrument or voice.

These organizations enable you to meet other teachers and to exchange ideas and solutions to teaching problems. Some groups sponsor local music festivals or competitions for students. Some are affiliated with state or national groups that have organized teacher training and certification programs.

The more active groups will gather at least once a month, often for a luncheon or dinner meeting. Membership dues and eligibility requirements vary with each group. Your local music dealer is usually able to provide information on these teacher organizations.

5. There are many instructional books available to keyboard teachers. Because of the specialized nature of the subject, helpful books are more likely to be found in a college library than in a public library.

6. Music magazines with emphasis on keyboard information, such as *Clavier, Keyboard Companion, Piano & Keyboard, Piano Guild Notes*, and *Sheet Music* are also helpful sources. Your local music store or public library may be able to provide sample copies or tell you where they may be obtained.

7. Recitals, concerts and other musical events offer opportunities to enrich your background as a teacher. Attending grade school and high school performances will help you keep attuned to local musical interests and achievements. Colleges, conservatories and churches offer many performances at modest cost. If your town does not offer any professional concerts, you can ask to be put on the mailing lists of colleges or concert halls in nearby cities.

CHAPTER 5

PSYCHOLOGY of TEACHING

Psychology involves sensitivity to the feelings of others, being a good listener, and the use of common sense. During the first six to eight weeks of lessons you will have to become acquainted with the "real person" inside each student — child, teen, or adult. Here are some guidelines that will assist in handling different situations.

A shy, quiet pupil may be very sensitive to criticism and will need a cautious, velvet glove approach. An outgoing, active, or aggressive person will need their energies directed carefully and may need firm or sometimes stern handling. Be aware that an aggressive person does not necessarily possess inner self-confidence. An outer shell of a lion may cover a kitten.

Talented students often seem deceptively easy to teach. They catch on quickly and usually need little encouragement. However, you must be sure that they are *really* learning to read notes and are not simply playing by ear. They need a constant challenge to avoid becoming bored. A clever but lazy student may attempt to deceive you with imaginative excuses for lack of progress. See Chapter 38, "Good Musical Ear: Problems and Blessings."

Be alert to differing attention spans. Generally, the younger the student, the shorter their attention span. At age 5 or 6 it may be only three or four minutes. Mood also affects a student's ability to concentrate. Students who are tired, or have other things on their mind will have shorter attention spans. You must be ready to switch from one piece to another or one book to another to avoid loss of attention.

Those with limited musical abilities will need more patience. You will often have to explain the same thing several different ways to make it understood. Some concepts may take two, three, or more weeks to "soak in."

You will probably encounter enthusiasm, sadness, anger, apathy, stubbornness and other moods that sometimes leave you with a feeling of bewilderment. These reactions can be caused by many factors, and usually have nothing to do with you personally. Perhaps the day at school has gone badly because of peer pressure or a low grade on a test. The student may have lost a dearly loved pet. Home life may have been disrupted by separation or divorce. Any number of other problems could be on his/her mind when coming to the lesson. Teenagers, especially, may have noticeable changes of mood. The change sometimes continues for weeks or even months. This requires special patience, stability and understanding from the teacher.

This is where you must be willing to lend an ear. Simply listen sympathetically and try to provide some encouragement, if possible. Occasionally, five minutes or so may be needed at the beginning of a lesson for the student to get things off his/her chest so the remainder of the lesson time will be more productive. However, be on the lookout for lazy students who attempt to cover up their lack of practice with unnecessary talking.

Above all, be genuine and sincere in what you do. Don't try to bluff your way through things. Children are especially quick to detect insincerity. If you don't know the answer, or are not sure, simply admit it, but say that you will find the answer and then search for it diligently.

HOW TO ACQUIRE
and KEEP STUDENTS

CHAPTER 6

HOW TO ACQUIRE STUDENTS

What Is the Best Age To Start a Student?

A good rule of thumb is that music study can begin any time after a child has completed first grade. By this time, most children have sufficient development of muscular coordination to learn the keyboard with ease. The reading and mathematics skills learned in the classroom along with the self-discipline experiences of homework and project completion are a distinct advantage when undertaking private music study. This is quite a safe guideline but one that is considered very conservative by some educators.

Very young children, age 4-5-6, have been taught successfully for many years. It has now been proven via many studies that the human brain takes in more knowledge from birth to age five than any other comparable time in life. Many kindergarten children are now reading books previously used in 1st or 2nd grade. One advantage is that their minds are fresh and uncluttered with daily planning, current events, peer pressure, etc. They also have more spare time available, without committments to after school sports, scouts and other activities.

In recent years, more and more adults are taking up piano study. Some are complete beginners, others are continuing after a lapse of many years from childhood study. There is really no upper age limit for piano study except for physical problems such as arthritis.

The age of the pupils you accept also involves a personal choice. For example, you may not feel comfortable with a wiggly four-year old, have difficulty relating to teen-agers, or are hesitant about teaching adults who are older than you. A lack of experience with a specific age group, however, should not necessarily limit your teaching. The cliche, "try it, you'll like it," has relevance. This book contains separate chapters with practical advice on the teaching of age 4-5-6 (Chapter 34), teen-agers (Chapter 35), and adults (Chapter 36). Approach each student positively and give the teaching your best efforts.

Obviously, your first need will be to "spread the word" that you are available for teaching. The rate of growth in the number of your students will depend upon the extent and effectiveness of your publicity. The ideas suggested here will vary in cost. A good plan would be to start modestly with advertising that involves small expenditures. You will have to experiment to find the publicity that works best in your area. Several different ideas could be used simultaneously.

You may want to set aside a portion of the income from your first few students for future advertising. You probably will need to continue some form of advertising until you have all the students you want.

To be realistic, you can't expect to have more than a few students during the first six months of teaching. It may take a month or more before you get your first pupil. Eventually, your best form of advertising will be your teaching reputation, but this will take many years of conscientious effort. Many established teachers do not advertise at all. Word-of-mouth, passed from one friend and neighbor to another, is sufficient to keep their schedules filled.

The following are some of the steps you may take to recruit students:

1. Place a small, neatly lettered sign or card in prominent businesses in your city or town. Many places provide a large community bulletin board for this purpose. The post office, bank, laundromat, grocery, and drug stores are examples.

The size and format is often limited. Many places require notices to be dated and routinely remove those that are more than two weeks old. Other stores simply clear off their entire bulletin board every few weeks. However, there is no reason for not going back and putting up another card later. Find out the details from the store manager.

If you know anyone who works in a store or shop, ask if they could help you get permission to put a sign or card in the front window. This is even better than a bulletin board.

The sign does not have to be elaborate or costly. A neat, do-it-yourself job is acceptable. If you have a home computer with typography or graphics software, you can design your own sign. Otherwise, a cut down poster board with rub-on letters or stick-on letters may be used. These are obtainable at stores with a school supply, stationery or art department. This will take a little time on your part, but it is worthwhile. Remember, the neatness of your card or sign is the first impression people will have of you.

The wording plays an important part in "selling yourself" to the public. "Wanted, Keyboard Students" is not too impressive. Make it sound as if it would be a privilege to take lessons from you. The following example might give you some ideas.

<u>NOTICE</u>
I am now accepting
PIANO and ORGAN STUDENTS
at my studio.
For complete information call 555-3210
between 11:00 am and 7:00 pm
Monday through Friday.
Mrs. Jane Doe • 111 Melody Lane • Yourtown

2. A sign could be placed on your front lawn, near your mail box, on the outside of your house, or in your front window. However, check with your city or town clerk to be sure that such a sign would be permitted by zoning ordinances. There may be laws regulating the size and placement of outdoor or indoor signs.

The sign will attract more attention if you use imagination and originality. Use weather resistant materials such as painted wood, plastic or metal. Plastic or metal letters are available in different sizes and colors from hardware or marine supply stores. Examples are shown on the next page.

3. Business cards are an excellent way to advertise. The cost is usually reasonable. One little card, in the right place at the right time, can produce a student for you. The more cards you get in circulation the better.

Distribute business cards to friends, relatives, social clubs, school groups, scout groups, and religious organizations. Music teachers (band, orchestra, and chorus) in nearby public and private schools are good people to contact. Music stores are often willing to post a business card or to take a dozen or more cards to distribute. Music dealers usually welcome them because they can lead to an increase in music sales and the possible sale of pianos and organs later.

There are many musical "logos" (small sketches or designs) that are available when ordering business cards. They make the card more attractive and eye-catching. Business cards are often supplied with a little plastic carrying case that fits nicely into your pocket or purse.

Business cards may be ordered at a print shop, wedding supply store, or stationery store. Be sure to get a written estimate of the cost in advance. Ask to look over a "proof" *before* the cards are printed. Read the proof very carefully. If anything is misspelled or omitted, this is your last chance to correct it without additional expense.

4. Become musically involved in community affairs. This will increase your visibility to the public and enhance your reputation as a musician. Most opportunities will be as a volunteer, but you may get a few paid jobs. Some possibilities are playing for church weddings, accompanying soloists and ensembles (especially when there are contests or auditions for junior high and high school students), and performing for private clubs, social groups, nursing homes, etc. Service clubs such as Kiwanis, Rotary, Optimist, etc. may need an accompanist for meetings that involve group singing. Sometimes a local mortuary is in need of an organist, when the family has no preference.

Obviously, some of this volunteer work will require extra time for planning, practice, and occasional rehearsals. Consider these efforts as one means of publicity, an investment in your future teaching career and a service to the community.

The way to start is by visiting various organizations and offering your services either as a substitute or as a volunteer. For example, you could offer to provide a 30-minute program of entertainment at a retirement home. A sing-along program might be effective. The same program could be offered to a different retirement home at a later time. For maximum publicity, you could arrange for a short newspaper article telling about your volunteer work.

5. Many cities have a "welcome wagon" or similar organization in the community. You could arrange to put a notice in the welcome basket given to each new family. A clever idea is to have the notice cut out in the shape of a note, grand piano, or other musical design. This would be an opportunity to offer a free introductory lesson (see section 8, below).

6. If you are a member of a church, ask to have a short notice added to the church newsletter or bulletin. The notice might be repeated again later. A sample is shown below.

Mrs. Jane Doe is now accepting children and adults
for private piano and organ lessons in her home.
Call 555-3210 for more information.

7. Public and private schools often have variety shows,
band concerts, operettas and musical shows where advertising space is available in the program. A simple ad could
be a reproduction of your business card.

8. A *free introductory lesson* is an excellent idea for a beginning teacher and for a teacher who has moved to a new
community. This free lesson could be mentioned in all of
the advertising you do – even on your business card.

The introductory lesson should be 20 to 30 minutes long.
If the prospective student is a beginner, introduce the keyboard by showing how letter names are associated with the
keys. Teach one or two short letter-name melodies. Discuss
what he/she hopes to gain from keyboard study. The most
important point you can make is how the enjoyment of music
will enrich the student's life. As a conclusion, you should
play a showy piece, intended to demonstrate your skill and
musicianship and, hopefully, to motivate the student to start
study with you!

If the prospective student has previously taken lessons,
ask him/her to bring along some old music to play. Determine the student's level of achievement by having him/her
do sight reading for you.

9. Try a small classified ad in a newspaper. The most economical is a weekly or biweekly community paper or shopping handout. You could also advertise in the paper of a
neighboring community. Often, the same company prints
both papers and you may get a reduced price when advertising in both. A big city daily newspaper is usually quite
expensive and reaches readers who are not likely to be pros-
pects simply because of distance.

Plan to have the ad repeated several times, at least once
a week for four weeks. The rates are often cheaper for rep-
etitions. The best times for advertising coincide with the

beginning of the public school semester in late August or early September and again in January.

Your local paper can suggest a classification such as "School, Instruction," "Music," or "Services Offered." A possible ad could be worded like this:

Piano and Organ Instruction.
Free Introductory Lesson. 555-3210

Optional extra lines are shown below.

Adults, Teens and Children.
Beginners and Intermediate.
Day or Evening.

10. Once you have made a commitment to keyboard teaching, you may want to place a listing in the *Yellow Pages*. This is published just once a year. The advertising should be placed about *6 months in advance* of the publication. An extra charge is usually added to your monthly phone bill for one year. Your local phone company can provide details.

"Music Instruction, Instrumental" is usually the appropriate classification. A simple one or two line listing, depending on the length of your name and address, would be most economical. This is a sample:

Jane Doe Keyboard Studio
123 Your St. • 555-3210

CHAPTER 7

HOW to KEEP STUDENTS

As you gain students, an important concern is to adopt attitudes and procedures that will encourage your students to study with you for as long as they can.

CHALLENGE, BUT NOT OVERWHELM.
One of the secrets of effective teaching is to help your students be successful most of the time. This is done is small steps. You want to challenge students sufficiently to keep their interest, but not overwhelm them with something too difficult. It is through a series of successes, even if small, that students gain confidence in themselves and are motivated to continue keyboard work.

MATCH MUSIC and PERSONALITY.
Your choice of supplements should be influenced by an individual's special interests and musical taste. If a child likes animals, pick out animal music. If the student likes jazz, find jazz for his/her level. The *Schaum Teachers Guide* has a classified index with many categories to help you locate the right music.

BE SENSITIVE to PERSONAL FEELINGS.
Be genuinely interested in each student, both as a person and as a musician. This will mean adjusting your teaching when necessary to accommodate the ups and downs that are normal with most people.

MAINTAIN COMMUNICATION with PARENTS.
Keep routine contact with parents through the lesson assignment book and *Student Report Sheet*. However, if there is a special situation, get on the phone. For example, if it is apparent that a student has not practiced for two weeks, contact the parents promptly. Try to find out if this is a temporary problem, or if it is something more deep-seated. In the long run, it is better to be frank and discuss any difficulties openly.

BE OPTIMISTIC and GENEROUS with PRAISE.
A cheerful, enthusiastic attitude is contagious! Students look forward to lessons when they are likely to find an optimistic and supportive atmosphere. Praise helps build confidence. Confidence helps build success. Success helps generate more success.

PRACTICAL ASPECTS
of TEACHING

CHAPTER 8

SCHEDULE ORGANIZING

It's a good idea to determine in advance, the times you wish to devote to teaching. Whether you live alone, share an apartment, live with your family, or are married, the times set for teaching music should be compatible with the activities of others in the household. If you have very young children, a baby sitter may be needed. If there are older children involved, their activities must be considered. Obviously, your family's needs should take priority over your teaching, but it often requires striking a balance or making a compromise.

Privacy is of utmost importance when teaching. The times you select to teach should be quiet and uninterrupted. Others in your household, especially children, must understand this. If you have an answering machine or voice mail, be sure it is activated, preferably to respond after the first ring. Otherwise, get someone else to answer your phone and take messages. The telephone should not interrupt a lesson unless it is an emergency. If you must talk on the phone during a lesson, make it as brief as possible.

If you have small children, look for a capable baby sitter. The sitter should be familiar with your daily routine and where things are located in the house. The sitter, of course, can answer the phone and should be instructed to write down all messages in full.

The times you teach will depend partly upon the ages of your students. After school and early evening times are usually best. Preschoolers and adults may be able to come at other times.

At first, try to schedule your lessons for the same day, preferably in sequence. If you need to tidy up the house or to change clothes in preparation for teaching, obviously it's easier to do this just once a day.

You should keep an accurate schedule at all times. This becomes more important as the number of your students increases. At first, an ordinary calendar with write-in space will be sufficient. If your schedule is important to others in the household, use a wall calendar in plain view to all.

SCHAUM LES	
MONDAY	TUESDAY
7:30	
8:00	
8:30	
9:00	
9:30	
10:00	
10:30	
11:00	
11:30	
12:00	
1:00	
1:30	
2:00	
2:30	
3:00	
3:30	
4:00	
4:30	
5:00	
5:30	
6:00	
7:00	
7:30	
8:00	
8:30	
9:00	
9:30	
10:00	

The Schaum *Lesson Schedule Card* is an inexpensive, pocket-size card with space for 30 minute lesson periods. Larger schedule books with a calendar are available at stores with a stationery department. If you have a home computer, you may want to use software for keeping track of your schedule.

When you have a schedule with five or more students in succession, you may want to consider a five minute buffer period between each lesson. This means allowing 35 minutes for each 30 minute lesson. For example, if you start teaching at 3:30, the lessons that follow will be scheduled to begin at 4:05, 4:40, 5:15, 5:50, etc. Although the times are not as easy to remember as every hour and half hour, parents and students are easily able to make the adjustment. The buffer time gives you many advantages.

The extra five minutes between lessons is your personal time to use any way you like. If you need a break for yourself, you can take a few minutes for a cup of coffee, make a phone call or start supper without cutting into anyone's lesson time. When you like, you can give a few minutes extra time to one student without worrying about running late. This scheduling has been used at the Schaum Music School for many years. Our teachers have found that it relieves the stress of trying to maintain back-to-back 30 minute lessons and that they rarely run behind schedule. For parents and students, it means that they always get a full 30 minute lesson. Also see Chapter 13, Section F. Lesson Appointments.

CHAPTER 9

HOW MUCH to CHARGE
for LESSONS

You will have to make your own decision regarding the price you charge for lessons. There are seven important factors to consider (see sections A through G on the following pages). These will require some soul searching and honest answers to the questions in each section which all relate to the price you set.

Your lesson fee should increase as you gain more experience, enhance your reputation, and add to your musical training. Be sure to re-evaluate these factors every one or two years. The cost of living and economic inflation in your area must also be considered. Many teachers are reluctant to increase their lesson fee for fear of losing students. However, if fee increases are reasonable, there are actually very few students who will quit. If you think there is a genuine hardship and the student is musically talented, you could make a special exception. A logical time to change your fee is at the beginning of a new semester or at the beginning of a year. A written notice, sent out at least 30 days in advance, is both businesslike and helpful.

Most lesson fees for private teachers are for a 30 minute lesson. If you plan to give 40, 45 or 60 minute lessons, the price should be adjusted accordingly.

When there is more than one student in the same family, you may want to slightly reduce your fee for the 2nd and 3rd (or more) students. This "family discount" could be 50 cents or one dollar less per lesson.

A. LOCAL COMPETITION

What are other keyboard teachers in your neighborhood charging for lessons? What does your local music store charge for keyboard lessons? How does your training, experience and versatility compare to that of other teachers? How close to you is the nearest keyboard teacher? If you're the only teacher within 10 or 15 miles, you may be able to charge more than otherwise. Generally, teachers in rural areas and small towns charge less than teachers in larger cities.

B. FORMAL MUSIC TRAINING

How many years have you had private keyboard lessons? Are any of your teachers well-known, especially in the locality where you are teaching? Have you had any college or conservatory classes? Do you have a degree in music? Is your college or conservatory well-known in your area? Generally, the more training you have had, the more you can charge for lessons.

C. TEACHING EXPERIENCE

How long have you been teaching keyboard? Have you also taught other instruments or voice? Have you done any classroom teaching in a public school? Have you worked with children or adults in groups such as Scouts or Sunday School? Any experience involving handling of people, especially children, is helpful and contributes to your worth as a private teacher.

D. RANGE of AGES

Do you feel comfortable teaching a five or six year old child? Do you feel comfortable teaching 7th and 8th graders or high school students? Do you feel comfortable teaching someone your own age or someone 10 or 20 years older than you? Usually, you can ask a higher fee when you are able to teach a wider range of ages.

E. RANGE of MUSIC LEVELS

Do you like to teach beginners? Are you comfortable teaching Level Three and Level Four? Level Five and Level Six? Are you comfortable preparing an advanced high school student for a contest or audition? Are you comfortable preparing a student for music college entrance auditions? Could you help a student who wants to accompany a choral group, violin solo or trombone solo? A teacher who can handle advanced students usually can get a higher lesson fee.

F. YOUR REPUTATION in the COMMUNITY

How long have you been teaching in the community? Have you just moved into town? Have you been teaching in the same area for 15-20 years? If you are new to the community, you will probably not be able to ask the same lesson fee as you had been getting before you moved.

Are you involved in community musical activities? Are you a church organist or choir director? Do you accompany students in contests and auditions? Do you play for any service club or lodge? Do you teach music in the public schools? Are you a member of a community orchestra, chorus or band? Have you performed on radio or TV? Do you have any music published? The greater your public exposure the more you will be able to ask for a lesson fee.

G. DO YOU OBTAIN MUSIC for YOUR STUDENTS?

Do you maintain a small stock of music in your studio, ready to give to your pupils? If so, the money you have invested in your music stock and the time you spend making trips to the music store or ordering through the mail is a service that is valuable and convenient for your students. Parents, then, do not have to make trips to a music store. The continuity of lessons is not interrupted because of a lack of music.

Some teachers add a small amount (perhaps 25¢) to their weekly lesson fee to cover the cost of supplying music. Others add a "service charge" of $3.00 to $5.00 per semester for each student to cover the costs of obtaining music and also any awards you may want to give. If parents object, simply ask them to obtain the music as needed. After a few trips to the music store they'll find out that your "service charge" is a bargain.

When selling music to your students, they should be expected to pay the full price plus sales tax, the same as they would if they purchased it at a store. This should be done even if you have received a discount on the music.

CHAPTER 10

STUDIO LAYOUT

It is assumed that you will use your home when you begin teaching. The choice of room and placement of the keyboard should be planned for maximum privacy — away from others in the household, T.V., and other activities. It's very important that your students not have any distractions.

You will need an end table, TV tray, or short file cabinet at one side of the keyboard where you plan to sit. Use it for pencils, award seals, etc. (see Chapter 11, "Supplies for Teaching"). The idea is to avoid getting up and down during the lesson, thus disturbing the student's concentration. Be sure the keyboard is well lighted, especially if the room has little natural illumination. The student should not be able to look out the window when seated at the keyboard. A curtain, window shade, or shutter will serve very nicely to eliminate this possibility.

If you will be teaching very young children, you should have a seat cushion to help the child maintain good posture and the right height for a proper hand position at the keyboard. A pillow, thick book, or sofa cushion will work in a pinch.

The fun of decorating around your keyboard need not be expensive. Music plaques, cardboard cut-outs, magazine pictures, or a bulletin board are all possibilities. You want to provide a pleasant musical atmosphere which will make students look forward to their lessons.

The ideal situation is to have a separate waiting room for parents, brothers, sisters, and friends. You will have much more success when you and the student are alone together — without having an audience to express visible reactions or interference. This waiting room could be another room in your house, a hallway, enclosed porch, etc. with space for at least two persons to sit. If very young children are likely to be in the waiting room, keep safely out of reach

your breakables and anything that might cause an inju-
ry. You should provide books and magazines to amuse both
adults and children while they wait. If it is impossible to
have a separate waiting room, a folding screen or curtain
might be used as a room divider.

*Mrs. Higgins, we just got a great deal on a piano!
When can you fit Penelope in your schedule?*

CHAPTER 11

SUPPLIES for TEACHING

The following supplies are suggested when you start teaching. You may already have many of them. The more expensive items may be purchased later as your budget permits.

ESSENTIAL ITEMS:

Calendar

Clock or Watch

* Lesson Schedule Card

Metronome

* Music Dictionary

* Music Flash Cards

Paper Clips

Pencils

Rubber Bands

Scissors

Scotch Tape

* Stars or Award Stickers

OPTIONAL ITEMS:

Bulletin Board

Calculator

Chalk Board / Chalk

Felt Pens

File Cabinet

* Gold Award Seals ‡

Paper Punch

Pencil Sharpener

Cassette Recorder / Tapes

Rubber Stamp / Ink Pad

Ruler

Set of Balls: ping pong, handball, tennis, hardball
(for shaping hand position, see Chapter 13, Section B)

Shelves for Music and Books

Stapler / Staples

CD Player

---

* Published by Schaum Publications, Inc.
(See Chapter 46, "Teaching Aids, Dictionaries, etc.")

‡ For end of book and award certificates

CHAPTER 12

RECORD KEEPING

Just like your doctor, dentist or other professional, you should keep records of each student's attendance, payments, music purchased and an evaluation of progress. The *Music Teacher's Organizer*, published by Schaum Publications, Inc., is an ideal way to organize your records. This packet includes several pads with sheets that can be torn off as needed for each student:

1. *Student History and Record Sheet*
   Used to record the complete background of the student

2. *Student Report Sheet*
   An incentive grading system for use by teacher, student, and parents

3. *Studio Policy and Rules*
   Given to parents at the first lesson to explain rules on missed lessons

4. *Comprehension Quiz*
   Used to determine the knowledge of a transfer student or as a progress quiz

The packet also includes a listing of items which may qualify for income tax deductions. Since tax laws vary in each state, and since other circumstances may affect your tax status, the final determination should be made with the advice of a qualified tax consultant.

If you have a home computer, you may want to use it for keeping some student records. Simple word processing software would probably be sufficient. Your computer may also be used for keeping financial records. See Chapter 45, "Computer Possibilities."

RELATIONSHIPS of TEACHER, STUDENT, and PARENTS

CHAPTER 13

ESSENTIAL HABITS
to ESTABLISH

This chapter is divided into these sections:

A. POSTURE and SEATING POSITION

At the beginning of the first lesson, the student must be shown how to sit up straight. It is preferable to sit on the front part of the bench or chair. This permits freedom of arm, leg and body movement, which becomes increasingly important as the student progresses. Sitting near the front of the bench allows students with short legs to reach the pedals of the piano or organ more easily.

Seating height should be adjusted with a cushion or thick book. The object is to raise the body so that the underside of the forearms is nearly level with the keyboard. This will put the wrist and hand into place where a good hand position can be established. Obviously, a similar cushion or thick book should be used at home when practicing.

Don't worry if a child's feet are unable to reach the pedals. At first, it is more important to establish the proper hand position and seating posture. At the piano, the damper pedal is not used until Level 2. At the organ, start with manuals only and add pedals later.

B. HAND POSITION

After posture and seating position are shown, a good hand position should also be established at the first lesson. Most teachers agree that fingers 2-3-4-5 are to be curved. When curved, the fingers should form an approximately straight line when placed on the white keys. See the illustration in Chapter 27, "First Lesson." This resembles the formation of the hand and fingers needed to catch a ball.

Depending on hand size, grasping a ping pong ball, handball, tennis ball or baseball (hardball) will bring fingers into proper position. Having these balls available for use in your studio is recommended.

It is best to press the keys with the tips of fingers 2-3-4-5. This assumes that fingernails are trimmed properly, which may be a problem with teens and adults. It is possible to play with longer fingernails, but the altered hand position is not the best for getting maximum leverage. It limits control and strength at the keyboard.

C. WRISTS, ARMS and ELBOWS

Wrists should be held so they are nearly level, parallel to the keyboard. A good test is to place a large coin or bottle cap on the back of the hands. The coin or cap should not slide off when the keys are played.

Efficiency of movement and conservation of physical energy are important aspects of keyboard playing. Wasted and unneeded movements make playing not only more awkward, but unnecessarily tiring. In the long run, these wasted movements will impede both dexterity and endurance.

The wrist should have relatively little vertical movement while playing. Constantly moving the wrist up and down, like a pump handle, is a common example of wasted movement.

Movement of the forearm and elbow should also be minimized. Exaggerated side-to-side elbow movement is not needed to achieve a good phrase release. This "elbow flapping" is another common example of wasted movement and energy.

D. PRACTICE HABITS

Whether a new beginner or transfer student, 6 year old or 66 year old, you must make clear your expectations to your student for practice between lessons. A written record of the assignment and your practice aims are essential. See Chapter 14, "Practice Habits for Students."

E. PAYMENT of LESSON FEES and MUSIC

The best plan is to get payment of one month's lessons in advance, with payment due no later than the first lesson of each month. This should be clearly understood before the first lesson is scheduled.

Also explain that the music you provide must be paid by the first lesson of the following month, along with the monthly lesson fee. When selling music to your students, make clear that you expect them to pay the full price plus sales tax, the same as they would if they purchased it at a store. (This should be done even if you have received a discount when buying the music.)

You're not helping anyone by being late in collecting money that is rightfully yours. Asking for prompt payment of the lesson fee and music helps maintain a respectful, businesslike and professional attitude on the part of parents - and adults who are paying for their own lessons.

For those who cannot afford to pay for an entire month in advance, insist on payment at the beginning of every lesson. Music should be paid for at the lesson one week after it is given to the student. Don't let payments get behind; it's much easier for the student to find the money for one lesson than it is for two or three.

F. LESSON APPOINTMENTS

Starting lessons on time is an obvious virtue. You should make every effort to avoid circumstances that would cause you to be late. If you have scheduled a 30 minute lesson, the student is entitled to a full 30 minutes. Occasionally, you may want to give a student a few minutes extra lesson time, but it should never make you late for the next student. Some teachers feel more comfortable leaving five or ten minutes buffer time between lessons, rather than scheduling back-to-back.

Remember, many students have to be chauffeured. If the lesson time is not predictable, it will be annoying to parents who are trying to fit in the trip to and from the lesson with other family activities.

There's also a simple psychology at work. If the teacher takes a careless attitude toward appointments and length of lesson periods, it is usually reflected by a similarly careless attitude toward music study by parents and children. This is certainly not a good atmosphere for learning and will eventually have a detrimental effect on the teacher's reputation.

G. MISSED LESSONS and TARDINESS

As with payments, your attitude toward missed lessons and tardiness must be businesslike. When you schedule a lesson, you are reserving your time for a specific student. A keyboard lesson is not a casual social meeting; it is a professional appointment. When a student is late or does not show up, your time is either wasted or used inefficiently.

You want to establish a policy that will be fair and yet not tolerate those who are habitually late or who miss lessons for frivolous reasons.

Handling tardiness is quite easy. Students who arrive late simply get only the remaining time left in the lesson period. If you have no lesson scheduled afterward, you may be tempted to give a few minutes extra time as compensation for the tardiness. However, you must judge the reason for being late and also any previous tardiness. If you are lenient, the student may assume that they get a full 30 minute lesson whether they arrive on time or not!

A policy on missed lessons requires careful thought and should be written down. This could be combined with your policy on lesson payments. A copy, duplicated on a copy machine, should be given to each new student before lessons are started.

Depending upon the reason, some missed lessons can be made up at a later time, whereas others should not. Here are some guidelines:

1. *Reasons.* You must decide the circumstances that are acceptable for an "excused" lesson. Any illness or family emergency may be excused. Otherwise, you would only excuse lessons for vacation time several weeks per year. Certainly, you will not excuse a lesson if the reason is to see the neighbor's new puppy, to go shopping, or go to a movie.

2. *Advance Notice.* Common courtesy requires that you be notified as soon as possible if a lesson appointment cannot be kept. In case of illness, accident, or family emergency, it is reasonable to accept notice within 4 to 24 hours before the lesson. Obviously, if a child has just broken a wrist within a few hours before the lesson, you may accept less advance notice. However, unless illness is of a sudden nature or emergency, if you get notification just 30 minutes before lesson time, you are justified in not excusing the lesson. When a child is ill, the

symptoms are usually evident early enough to enable parents to give you at least 4 hours advance notice.

If the student's family is going on vacation, you may expect to be told at least two to three weeks ahead of time. Other circumstances may require one to two weeks advance notice.

3. *Paying for Missed Lessons.* If a lesson is excused, you will keep the payment (if made in advance), but allow the student to make up the lesson later, at your convenience.

If a lesson is not excused, or if you have not been notified within a reasonable time in advance, you are justified in keeping the lesson payment and not permitting a make-up.

Obviously, there's a big advantage to getting your money in advance. However, even if the student is paying for the lesson each week, you have a right to ask for payment for an unexcused absence.

H. DISCIPLINE

Initial relationships between teacher and child set the pace for the future. During the first three or four lessons, important attitudes, reactions, and expectations are established. At this stage, discipline problems are relatively easy to control if appropriate action is taken promptly.

A simple guideline is to reward good conduct and good work and to overlook all but the worst. It pays to have a good sense of humor, take a joke gracefully, and be even-tempered. Students enjoy sharing a funny story, or even an occasional practical joke. When this is done good-naturedly and without harm, it may be considered a compliment. After all, the student would not be sharing humor if he/she didn't care about you. Most students will seldom cause any problems.

There are some children and teens who purposely try to test a teacher's patience and tolerance. Occasionally, they attempt to shock you with their language or behavior. They hope to irritate you, upset you and make you an unwilling audience for their antics. Here are a few examples:

Being purposely inattentive

Pretending to be forgetful

Making jokes, trying to be funny or cute

Interrupting with irrelevant remarks or questions

Using distracting gestures and movements

Using crude or foul language

You can usually tell if such testing is good-natured or vindictive. If the problem is only mildly irritating, simply ignore it; don't let it appear to bother you. It will likely "die on the vine." However, if the circumstances are quite annoying and disruptive, you will have to be assertive - the sooner the better. Usually a firm reprimand, "I don't permit that language [or behavior] here," is sufficient. Make threats only if you are able and willing to carry them out. An obviously empty threat will weaken your position. Certainly, do not use any physical punishment. Persistent or extreme cases should be reported to parents promptly.

Occasionally, parents who naively believe their child can do no wrong will decline to help resolve a discipline problem. In such cases it is usually better to terminate lessons - the sooner the better. Without parent cooperation, attempting to handle an unruly or uncooperative child is futile.

Also consult Chapter 5, "Psychology of Teaching."

I. INTERRUPTIONS DURING LESSONS

It is the teacher's responsibility to minimize outside interruptions during lessons. Several ideas have been presented in Chapter 8, "Schedule Organizing," and in Chapter 10, "Studio Layout."

The most common distractions during lessons are the telephone and doorbell. If possible, have someone else attend to them while you are teaching. If you can afford it, you might consider a telephone answering machine to use during the time you teach.

Adult students are often annoyed by disturbances, especially those which demand your time during the lesson. If there have been unavoidable interruptions which have taken time away from the lesson period, offer to give extra make-up time when it is convenient.

J. INTERFERENCE from PARENTS

As a teacher, you want to encourage parental support, which can make a big difference in the success and progress of a child. This is discussed in Chapter 15, "Parents' Role." However, overanxious or overprotective parents can be an impediment to your teaching.

Sometimes, parents try to impose their own, perhaps frustrated, musical ambitions on their child. Or maybe they want their child to emulate a musical neighbor, friend, or peer. They are so anxious for the child to be successful with music that they push too much, are too demanding of perfection in practice, or try to give extra lessons at home. This well-meaning but misguided interference can seriously undermine your teaching efforts and relationship with the child.

You certainly don't want the parents to be second-guessing your teaching. Their attempts may confuse the child with explanations that are unclear, incomplete, or conflict with yours. They may try to teach something that is too difficult, or for which there has been inadequate preparation. This situation requires a private conference, without the child. If they are not willing to let you be the teacher, and for you to decide what, when, and where things are to be presented, then it's time for you to resign and let them do their own teaching!

K. IF YOU'RE NOT SURE — DON'T GUESS!

A teacher should endeavor to be conscientious and truthful. This has been discussed in Chapter 1, "Qualifications and Ethics of Teaching," and in Chapter 5, "Psychology of Teaching." If you're not sure of what to do next, or how to answer a question, don't try to bluff your way through. It is very embarrassing as well as damaging to your credibility to be shown wrong after you have attempted to guess an answer.

In the long run, your reputation will be served far better by freely admitting when you don't know an answer but then working hard to find it.

Mrs. Higgins, I'm Johnny's Dad.
I understand you wanted to see me.

CHAPTER 14

PRACTICE HABITS
for STUDENTS

Most students and their parents have only a vague idea of how to practice. One mother, who brought her beginning eight year old daughter to the first lesson, naively asked, "How many *hours* a day should Sarah practice?" Sadly, many people associate music with long hours of dull, dreary practice. There are other parents who seem to feel that teachers have magical powers to make the child practice willingly and learn effortlessly, especially with no help from parents.

PRACTICE SCHEDULE. You have to educate both parents and students in good practice habits from the start. This applies both to new beginners and to *transfer students.* An excellent way is to ask parent and child to sit down together and work out a daily schedule of time available for practice. If the parents are involved in lots of activities, they already realize the value of a schedule. A good schedule will also help the child organize time for school work and other activities.

Practice does not always have to be at the same time every day. The schedule should allow for potential conflicts if the instrument shares a room with the TV or stereo. The schedule should be written down on paper and posted on the refrigerator door, where the whole family can see it.

Practicing six days a week is reasonable and allows one day off. Although Sunday is the most logical day off, it could be used as a make-up when practice cannot be done on a week-day. Once the schedule is established, it is up to the parents to see that it is maintained. It is especially important that parents enforce this practice schedule during the first three weeks of lessons — or until the practice times become routine.

IMPORTANCE of WRITTEN ASSIGNMENTS.

Both parent and child should clearly understand what is expected during daily practice. The best way is to provide a written record. One of the following is recommended:

Schaum *Progressive Practice Plans*

Schaum *Lesson Assignment Book*

Both of these provide space for you to write the page number or title of each piece to be practiced and room for the student to record his/her daily work. The *Progressive Practice Plans* also allows you to specify the *number of times per day* each piece is to be practiced. This is especially good for beginners. Start using an assignment book at the first lesson.

QUALITY NOT QUANTITY. The *quality* of practice is more important than the quantity of time spent. A surprising amount can be accomplished when full attention is focused on practice objectives, even for a short period of 10 to 15 minutes. This takes self-discipline and also means setting aside a quiet time, free from interruptions. Practice assignments should be goal oriented as much as possible.

The adage, "practice makes perfect," can be misleading. Simply spending time at the keyboard is not enough. Only *careful, accurate practice* makes "perfect." The quality of performance reflects the quality of practice.

HOW MUCH TIME for PRACTICE? Optimum practice time will vary with the individual student's age, motivation, ability to concentrate and musical level. Obviously, a beginner's pieces and assignments are quite short and do not need a lot of time. As a student advances and has longer and more difficult pieces, more practice time will be necessary.

For a young beginner (age 6 or 7), 10-15 minutes practice per day might be sufficient. Older students should be practicing 20-30 minutes per day. More advanced students and adults should be able to do 30-60 minutes per day.

TEMPO for PRACTICE. In learning a new piece, all students should start slowly, and gradually increase their practice tempo until reaching the performance tempo, as indicated by the tempo mark or metronome speed. It may take several weeks to achieve the performance tempo, depending upon the difficulty of the music, the time spent, and the quality of the practice.

METRONOME USE. A metronome helps determine the performance tempo, but may also be helpful in determining various practice tempos. A goal oriented assignment might be to increase the tempo to a specific speed during the course of a week's practice. The metronome is also valuable in teaching the feeling for a steady beat and learning new rhythms.

A student should not become dependent upon the metronome by using it too much. The goal should be to establish the feeling for a steady beat *within the student's mind and body,* without relying on a metronome.

LISTEN CAREFULLY. Training the ear to *listen carefully while playing* is an extremely important part of practicing. At first, students should be taught to listen for dynamics. As they advance, they should listen for rhythms, phrasing, damper pedal, etc.

AVOID INTERRUPTIONS and DISTRACTIONS. It should be explained to parents that the time spent at the instrument will be much more productive when sounds from TV, stereo, etc. are minimized or eliminated. Family pets, children and visitors should be out of sight, and if possible, out of hearing range. Parents can help by controlling potential distractions during practice time. A well planned practice schedule will help avoid distractions. If the student has an electronic instrument, headphones are ideal to mask out household noises.

PARENTAL ENCOURAGEMENT. The genuine interest of a parent is one of the strongest motivating factors a child can have. Simply checking on the practice schedule will help immensely. Devoting 10 to 15 minutes per week, giving *undivided attention* to the child's practice, demonstrates interest and concern. Also see Chapter 15, "Parents Role."

CHAPTER 15

PARENTS' ROLE

Parents play a big part in the success of every student. Unfortunately, there is often the feeling that just providing transportation and payment for lessons is all that is necessary. Many times a parent will say to you, "I don't know the first thing about music so I won't be able to give any help!" Right then is the time to let them know, emphatically, that they *can help* and that their help is *vital*. Parents need no musical knowledge to provide this support to your teaching.

1. Provide a Well-Maintained Instrument. The student's home piano or organ should be checked to be sure that all the keys, pedals, stops, and controls work properly. With the family's consent you can look it over yourself. If repairs seem to be needed, a music store can usually recommend a technician. It is advisable to get a written estimate of the repair costs in advance.

Piano tuning is recommended *at least* once a year. It's better if it can be tuned two times each year. To help stabilize the tuning, a piano should be kept against an inside wall, away from windows, radiators, and heating ducts.

Some organs also need tuning, especially older models. An organ dealer or electronic organ technician would be able to provide more information.

If the family is thinking about the purchase of an instrument, suggest that they consider rental plans or used instruments available from various music stores until it is more certain that the student's interest will be long lasting. An electronic keyboard may be better suited to a family's budget. However, they should be advised to get an instrument with at least a four octave range and *full size keys* (the same size as standard piano keys).

2. Keep Appointments Promptly. Parents are responsible for getting their child to your studio *on time* each week. You will have to establish rules for those who are late and for missed lessons. Guidelines are found in Chapter 13, Section G, and in the *Music Teacher's Organizer,* published by Schaum Publications, Inc.

3. Be Sure All Materials Come Along to Each Lesson. Parents should check that there are no missing books or other materials needed for each lesson. The lesson assignment book is especially important.

4. Pay Lesson Fees Promptly. Don't hesitate to *ask for money* that is rightfully yours! It is best to have a written policy explaining payment of lesson fees, music, and the handling of missed lessons. Suggestions are found in Chapter 13, Section E.

5. Encourage Regular Practice. Parents must help instill a sense of responsibility to finish what is started. They must reinforce your firmness in insisting on regular practice.

Establishing a specific time for practice each day is vitally necessary. Obviously, practice should not have to compete with the TV, stereo, or other family activities. The practice schedule should take these things into consideration.

For a child beginner, 10 to 20 minutes per day is usually sufficient. Teen and adult beginners are usually able to practice more because of longer concentration spans. As assignments become more difficult and pieces require more preparation, a longer practice time will be necessary.

6. Encouragement and Praise. At least once a week, parents should take time to listen to the practicing, giving it their full attention. The genuine interest of a parent, along with periodic praise and encouragement, is one of the best motivating factors a music student can have. This shows the child that the parents care and are proud of what is being accomplished.

7. Communication With the Teacher

Parents should be encouraged to speak with you if there are questions, problems, unusual home circumstances, or health situations that would affect practicing, attitude or progress. It is best to discuss such things privately (away from the student) and as soon as possible so that serious consequences or misunderstandings are avoided. If you sense unusual or persistent problems during the course of several lessons, you should initiate contact with the parent.

If marginal or unsatisfactory lessons are allowed to continue, some parents will *blame you* for their child's lack of progress or success. If you have worked hard to motivate and keep the child's interest (see psychology, Chapter 5) but with poor results, you should take the initiative and talk directly to the parent. Don't wait more than six or eight weeks. If the student (or parents) decide to stop the lessons there may be an unspoken blame on you which, via the grapevine, will do harm to your reputation as a teacher.

8. The Last Resort: How To Tactfully Stop Lessons

When you have exhausted all avenues and continue to find student apathy frustrating and taking the joy out of teaching, it is time to take action! Although this sample letter may seem cold and dispassionate, it usually produces parental respect for your professionalism.

Dear [parents name],

In looking over [student's name] (1) attendance record (2) progress (3) grades (4) attitude toward music [choose one or more reasons] during the past [four months], I feel he/she has lost interest in music lessons. Since we have discussed this previously, I'm sure you are aware that his/her priorities are on other things at this time.

I am really very sorry. As much as I have enjoyed working with [student's name] I feel we are not only wasting your money, but also taking my time that could be spent with another student who is eager to learn. Therefore, I think it best to discontinue lessons at this time.

I do hope that he/she will continue to play and utilize the skills and love for music learned thus far.

Respectfully,
[teacher's signature]

MUSICIANSHIP DEVELOPMENT

CHAPTER 16

CURRICULUM DEVELOPMENT

Ideally, before starting to teach, you should have in mind your musical objectives along with a step-by-step plan for accomplishing them with any level of student. An experienced teacher with full musical and academic training could certainly develop such a curriculum but it would be a long and laborious task. Without an extensive background, it is far better and much easier to adopt an established method as a time saver and for balanced, systematic progress.

Keyboard lessons should teach these important elements of musicianship:

1. **Note Reading:**
   The ability to explore new music.

2. **Finger Strength and Dexterity:**
   Vital for good keyboard technique.

3. **Musical Style:**
   A variety of music from different periods.

4. **Music Appreciation:**
   Knowledge of composers and music history.

5. **Performance:**
   Poise and confidence when playing for others.

John W. Schaum has developed a progressive curriculum that embraces these elements of musicianship. It is based on his analysis of over 50 years' teaching experience. Sound musicianship, he feels, is attained by "making haste slowly" and staying on the same level until it is mastered. This is accomplished by finishing a minimum of one book in each of four categories. The Four-Book Plan is to be used at each level of study.

1. METHOD Book

2. THEORY Book

3. TECHNIC Book

4. REPERTOIRE Book

This Four-Book Plan should be tailored to each student's needs, depending upon ability and interests. For average students, one book in each category is usually sufficient. For slower learners, additional supplements may be necessary. The *Schaum Teachers Guide* offers you many choices within each category.

CHAPTER 17

Importance of
NOTE READING

Nearly all teachers agree that one of the most valuable skills that can be passed on to students is the ability to read notes fluently. Human nature strives toward independence. Pupils of all ages — preschoolers, grade schoolers, teen-agers, adults, even grandparents — take pride in and enjoy being able to do things *by themselves.* This is especially true with music.

The emphasis in Schaum's *Making Music at the Piano* method is on note reading. This is developed at the very beginning by a special "Touch-Finding Technique." Every level of the Schaum method focuses on note reading.

Students get great satisfaction and pleasure in being able to explore new music independently. Let this be one of your foremost aims! If you teach your pupils to read, they can educate themselves.

The Schaum *Keyboard Touch Finder.*

CHAPTER 18

Importance of the
SENSE of TOUCH

Most people are aware of the importance of ears and eyes in keyboard playing. However, the sense of sight is often overworked. The student learns finger numbers by looking; he/she learns the keyboard by looking; then comes notation – another big job for the sense of sight. The keyboard student is too busy looking! A common problem of many students is looking down at their hands and the keyboard most of the time. This habit inhibits the speed and accuracy of music reading.

Unfortunately, the sense of touch has been neglected in keyboard teaching. At the very start, the beginner should be taught to find middle C by touch only. This can be done by getting the feel of the black keys, which become the Braille of the keyboard. Similarly, finger numbers can be learned by touching the keys with various fingers.

The ultimate results are well worth the preliminary effort to adjust to this new approach. The student will be free to concentrate his/her vision on the music. The keyboard will be mastered through touch. Better music reading will be accomplished and the sense of hearing will be stimulated and cultivated.

In the primer level of *Making Music at the Piano*, John W. Schaum applies to his touch system the term "Blind Flying," familiar to today's pilots. The student is designated as "Piano Pilot 88," referring to the total number of keys on the piano. Mr. Schaum helps the beginner by supplying a *Keyboard Touch Finder*, a large printed sheet which slips over the pupil's head and under the music, covering the actual keyboard. The *Keyboard Touch Finder* has a printed keyboard showing the relationship of keys, fingers and printed notes.

CHAPTER 19

FINGER STRENGTH
and TECHNIC

To the casual viewer, professional athletes on TV make their sport seem deceptively simple. But most people realize that to become skilled in basketball, football, swimming, tennis and other athletics requires muscle conditioning, study, lots of practice, and the supervision of a coach. Athletes are continually exercising with calisthenics, weights, conditioning machines, and other practice routines beyond actual participation in their sport.

Watching a professional pianist or organist likewise makes the performance seem quite easy. Unfortunately, the average person has little appreciation of the training and skills involved. This is because when playing the keyboard, the hands, feet, and body have subtle movements involving many small muscles that are not particularly impressive to a casual viewer. The vital coordination of ears, eyes, and fingers is almost imperceptible. This is why most beginning keyboard students, especially adults, underestimate the effort, practice, and muscular development needed.

There is more physical skill involved at the keyboard than most people imagine. Movements of eyes, fingers, and feet are involved along with arms, legs, and torso. These physical motions must be integrated with careful listening. Keyboard playing involves just as much physical coordination and muscular development as any sport. A concert pianist playing a full length recital needs the demanding physical endurance and agility of a soccer player, the controlled strength (but not the brute force) of a football player, and the concentration and control of an expert golfer.

It is very helpful to explain to students that physical training and discipline are needed for both athletics and keyboard playing. As in sports, success at the keyboard requires effort in muscle conditioning, study, lots of practice, and the supervision of a teacher. Keyboard muscle conditioning is called *technic*. Point out that technic exercises are as important to the keyboard player as calisthenics and workouts are to the athlete.

It is recommended that easy technic work be started with beginners after just four to five weeks of study. This is necessary for students of all ages. The most important aim in early technic work is to start developing finger strength so that each individual finger of both hands can play equally loud. The strategy is to approach the keyboard from a position of strength. Strong fingers can be controlled to play a full range of dynamics from *pianissimo* to *fortissimo* when necessary. Weak fingers, however, can play only a very limited range. In more advanced levels, as the student progresses and continues to gain in strength, the dynamic range can be expanded to *fortississimo* and *pianississimo*.

Schaum *FINGERPOWER* is a series of seven books, beginning at Primer Level, dedicated to development of individual finger strength and equal dexterity in both hands. The *Schaum Piano Teachers Guide* lists additional technic choices.

CHAPTER 20

Importance of the
MIDDLE - C APPROACH

The Middle-C Approach to piano playing is the most time-tested method of keyboard teaching in existence. Note reading proceeds in a logical sequence radiating from the center of the music notation system (middle-C), expanding through both staffs and into leger lines.

In spite of many detractors, critics, and competitive systems such as the "multi-key approach" and various "quick-learn" gimmicks (learn-by-colors, learn-by-numbers, etc.), the Middle-C Approach continues to prevail because of its unparalleled success and thoroughness. It is probably the most widely accepted keyboard teaching system presently in use.

John W. Schaum's *Making Music at the Piano* series is a modern method combining the Middle-C Approach with the five-finger position which, of course, is the basic foundation of all fingering at the keyboard. This method incorporates refinements developed during fifty years of teaching at the Schaum Piano School in Milwaukee, plus many other practical ideas suggested by experienced teachers from all parts of the United States.

The Schaum Middle-C Approach stresses *note reading* and the *gradual* introduction of other key signatures. In the beginning, emphasis is placed on the key of C to assure a grasp of white key names and locations, and to develop basic five-finger dexterity. As other keys are presented, they are always kept within the student's note reading range. The primer level introduces the keys of F and G major. As the method unfolds, key signatures of two sharps, two flats, etc. are brought in, with others proceeding in logical, key-circle rotation. Corresponding relative minor keys are also included.

CHAPTER 21

ADVANTAGES of SIMPLIFIED ARRANGEMENTS

Every teacher has aspirations of grooming students to a level of proficiency at which they can play original music by great composers. This goal of playing original masterworks is unquestionably worthy. There are, unfortunately, several obstacles to overcome on the road toward this goal.

One problem is that there is almost no music by master composers written for students in Primer Level, Level One, and Level Two. As students advance further through Level Three, Level Four, etc., they find increasingly more original music by the great composers. In Level Seven and beyond, original masterworks are plentiful. The question is how to select music, especially at the early levels, that will prepare pupils for the great composers.

Eighty years ago, beginning students commonly spent most of their time on scales and exercises. This dull routine continued until they had developed adequate proficiency to begin original classics. It is now generally agreed that this procedure is outdated and that some way must be found to let keyboard students of any age play real music from the very start. One solution is to provide simple arrangements of folk tunes and nursery rhymes. These can hardly be criticized since the music was not written for the keyboard in the first place, but more probably created for the unaccompanied human voice. This music may be all right for a very young child, but is unacceptable for older children and adults. An older child and a grown man or woman want to start right in with music of mature appeal.

Another problem, especially with children, is that original classics often have little appeal unless the student's musical taste has been carefully developed. In these days of cable TV, video games, computers, and heavily-publicized professional sports, young students are looking for music with more glamour and excitement. They also enjoy playing familiar music that can be shared with their friends.

The music we choose for our pupils will, in the long run, help mold their musical taste — something of lifelong importance. One of the important aims of keyboard teaching is to expose our pupils to a wide range of musical styles, especially the classics.

It is important to begin contact with master composers quite early. This is because it requires a lot of experience and musical maturity to appreciate the classics. This process may extend over several years. We can't expect a child (or even many adults) with just a few months of study to enjoy Bach or Beethoven in its original form.

Our goal of introducing students to the classics very early is frustrated by the fact that there is almost no keyboard literature available for the early levels. There are basically two alternatives; you can use original music by educational composers or use simplified arrangements. Most progressive teachers use a thoughtful mixture of both.

Simplified melodies of the master composers are a logical solution and serve three very sound educational purposes. First, they enable students to experience and sample music of the classics at a much earlier level than possible with the originals. Second, they help to foster a love and appreciation of good music which prepares them for more serious music study later. Third, they make master themes available to many students who may never progress to the point where they can play the original. It is far better to have played a simplified melody by Mozart than to have played nothing by Mozart. This is a musical compromise for pedagogic purposes that is sometimes misunderstood.

An important consideration in introducing the classics is student motivation. There is a simple psychology here. Titles of pieces, illustrations, lyrics, and attractive cover designs, especially on sheet music, are very important to children and help motivate their progress. Original classical titles such as "Bouree," "Air," "Melody," and "Sonatina" have very little appeal, particularly to children. This is the reason that classic melodies are often retitled when simplified, although the original title is frequently shown as a subtitle.

Most children would tire of a steady diet of master composer melodies, no matter how easy or varied. Obviously, other styles need to be included in the musical fare. The Schaum *Making Music at the Piano* method books include many simplified classics in all levels of the series along with a tasteful variety of other musical styles. For teachers who want more emphasis on the classics, the Schaum *Classic Melodies* books serve to broaden the student's exposure to master composers in Level One and Level Two.

The *Schaum Piano Teachers Guide* has listings of several hundred sheet music pieces and also numerous supplementary books at various musical levels. There is a generous choice of music by master composers along with music of many other styles.

CHOOSING
TEACHING MATERIALS

CHAPTER 22

TEACHING MATERIALS

One of the most difficult problems for any new teacher is to become acquainted with the vast quantity and variety of teaching materials available. You want to be able to prescribe, much like a physician, just the right teaching material at the right time! This is not something you learn overnight. Fortunately, there are several ways to search out the resources. Here are some examples:

1. PUBLISHERS' CATALOGS.

Most catalogs contain descriptions and thematics (musical samples) of books and sheet music. However, it is especially helpful when materials are *organized by level* so that you can see the full range of methods and supplements that are available *at each level*. For example, in the *Schaum Teachers Guide* (*free to teachers), you will find methods, workbooks, theory, technic, repertoire, supplementary books, sheet music solos, duets and teaching aids for six different levels.

A big time saver found in some catalogs is a *classified index*. This index helps to find supplements to match student interests and special needs. Some of the index listings in the *Schaum Teachers Guide* are: Action, Animals and Birds, Big Notes, Both Hands in Treble Clef, Christmas, Circus, Classics, Cross Hands, Cut Time, Dissonance, Duets and Ensembles, Ethnic Music, Halloween, Jazz, Left Hand Melody, etc.

Some publishers also have specialty catalogs which provide more information and detail than their general catalog. For example, Schaum Publications, Inc. offers (*free to teachers) four specialty catalogs:

Syllabus for Methods   *Syllabus for Sheet Music*
Syllabus for Repertoire   *Syllabus for Theory & Technic*

* Call Toll Free: 800 786-5023

2. VISIT a WELL-STOCKED MUSIC STORE.

See Chapter 26, "Where to Obtain Music."

3. KEYBOARD TEACHER SEMINARS.

Valuable information may be gained by attending a seminar or workshop. Usually a music dealer or college acts as the host and sends out invitations. Any keyboard teacher is welcome whether they are prospective, new, or established. Be sure to ask that your name be added to the mailing list of several music stores and colleges for future seminars. Attending seminars is a good way to meet other teachers, exchange ideas, and find out about local musical organizations.

Schaum Piano Teacher Seminars are given periodically in nearly all parts of the country. The seminars are enlightening and entertaining. The clinicians are active teachers with vast experience using the Schaum teaching program. You will enjoy their performances and insights and gain many little tips and ideas that will add to your teaching skills.

4. SAMPLE MATERIALS.

Some publishers, such as Schaum Publications, Inc., have a limited number of free professional samples available. If you write and explain your teaching needs, a special selection can be made for you. Occasionally, there is an opportunity to obtain music on an introductory offer.

5. PERSONAL LIBRARY
of TEACHING MATERIALS.

There are three important reasons to have your own library of teaching materials:

      1) Your own Study and Refresher.

      2) Sales to Your Pupils As Needed.

      3) Sight-Reading for Transfer Students.

For a beginning teacher, it would be too expensive to purchase one of everything needed for each student level, but this can be done "poco a poco" (little by little).

The main advantage in having extra music on hand is that there is no delay in obtaining a particular book or piece of sheet music when needed for a student. Otherwise, you or the parents will have to wait until there is time to make a trip to the music store or order it by mail. If you are not close to a music store, or if you are unable to get prompt and reliable service from a dealer, your personal library is especially important.

This means, of course, that some of your money will be invested in music. You will want to choose very carefully and keep records of what you sell. As your library expands, you may also want to invest in filing folders and file boxes or a file cabinet. The time spent in organizing and record keeping for your library saves valuable lesson time and can save money, too.

Your time and expenses involved in selecting, obtaining, and stocking music for your students should be compensated. See Chapter 9, Section G, "Do You Obtain Music for Your Students?," and Chapter 13, Section E "Payment of Lesson Fees and Music," for additional information.

A set of method books is a basic essential in your library. For example, there are eight levels in the Schaum *Making Music at the Piano* method. It would be wise to have at least the *first six* levels on hand. This set of methods is needed if you get a transfer student (one who has studied previously with another teacher). At the first lesson, you will want such a student to sight-read to determine his level of proficiency. If you are not familiar with this method, it will give you the opportunity to study the pieces in each book and to acquaint yourself with the learning progression.

It is also advisable to have on hand the first four levels of the Schaum *Fingerpower* series along with theory books for the first four levels such as Schaum's *Theory Workbooks*.

As you go along, you can add a nice variety of repertoire supplements to your library. After you have explored them yourself, they can be assigned as needed. When choosing music, keep in mind that each student has his own preferences and vary your selections accordingly. Eventually, you will want to have on hand a variety of classics, sacred, pop, country, jazz, boogie, etc.

CHAPTER 23

BEGINNER'S INSTRUCTION BOOKS

The way a job is started is of utmost importance. As a teacher, you are like a house builder. There's a lot of study and planning to be done before you order the lumber, bricks, shingles, etc. The foundation should be made as strong as possible to support the rest of the structure, knowing that there will be much stress upon it in the coming years.

As a teacher, you also need to plan your students' musical education by laying a firm foundation! The choice of method book plays an important part in teaching musical fundamentals.

FOR AGES 4 to 6.

For too long we have underestimated the learning capacity of these little ones. The only prerequisites are that the child knows the first seven letters of the alphabet, can count to five, and has enough finger dexterity to play the keys one at a time. This is a delightful age; they are loving and respectful; their minds are fresh and alert.

The Schaum *KEYBOARD TALENT HUNT, Book 1* is especially designed for this age. The child learns music by reading letter names instead of notes. Nursery rhyme melodies and illustrations are provided. The companion workbook is Schaum's *KEYBOARD ALPHABET WORKBOOK.*

FOR AGES 7 to 11.

Schaum's *MAKING MUSIC at the PIANO, Primer Level* is recommended. This is the first in a series of eight progressive method books.

The unique advantage of this book is the way it develops the sense of touch and trains the student to keep eyes on the music and *not* to look down at the hands and keyboard. Flash cards, duet accompaniments, and rhythm drills make this a value-packed volume.

For AGE 10 to ADULT.

Although teens and adults must learn the same musical fundamentals as youngsters, they require a more mature approach. Schaum's *PIANO for ADULTS, Beginner Level* fulfills this need.

Now, more than ever, adults are searching for recreation, intellectual growth, and continued education. Music study provides a new challenge and a great sense of satisfaction while developing keyboard skills.

CHAPTER 24

USE of SUPPLEMENTS

A method book alone is not sufficient for thorough training. As with public school teachers, it is important to have a well-rounded curriculum. This is outlined in the *Schaum Piano Teachers Guide;* it is called the **Four - Book Plan:**

        1. **METHOD** Book

        2. **THEORY** Book

        3. **TECHNIC** Book

        4. **REPERTOIRE** Book

METHOD BOOK.
This has already been discussed in Chapter 23, "Beginner's Instruction Books."

THEORY BOOK.
A workbook or music speller provides valuable reinforcement of the many elements of music encountered in the method. Although you can explain and demonstrate at the keyboard, writing gives an added dimension to learning. In addition, it helps teach music manuscript writing.

It has been proven that if a person *writes* something, it will be retained 50% longer than if not written. This makes it worth the extra time taken during a lesson to assign and explain a theory book page. The actual written work should be done as homework.

There are several possible Schaum theory books for beginners. One of the first two is definitely needed; the third is very helpful but optional. A theory book should be started at the very first lesson, along with the method book.

1. *KEYNOTE SPELLER, Primer Level*

2. *THEORY WORKBOOK, Primer Level*

3. *RHYTHM WORKBOOK, Primer Level*

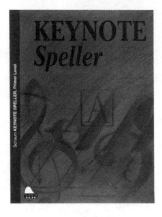

TECHNIC BOOK.

Finger dexterity and finger independence are very important ingredients of keyboard playing. Developing the necessary muscle control and coordination requires special training. This is provided by the Schaum *FINGERPOWER* books, which develop all five fingers of both hands.

It is usually best to wait four to six weeks before starting a technic book with a beginner. The recommended book is:

FINGERPOWER, Primer Level

REPERTOIRE BOOK.

Repertoire broadens the student's musical experiences beyond the method book. Method, theory, and technic books must be selected by you. However, in choosing repertoire materials, the student's interests and personal preference can be considered. It's an opportunity for "fun music."

A repertoire book should be assigned two or three weeks after the technic book. There are many choices within each level. Here are some popular primer level albums published by Schaum Publications, Inc.

CHRISTMAS PRIMER

FOLK SONG PRIMER

HYMN PRIMER

PATRIOTIC PRIMER

Additional selections are listed in the *Schaum Piano Teachers Guide.*

Most teachers consider method, theory, and technic to be the meat, potatoes, and vegetable of music study. Repertoire material is the dessert. A word of caution: sometimes, when the student is working on "fun music," preparation on the remainder of their books suffers. If a verbal warning is not effective, you may simply keep the favorite music in your studio until the assignments in the other, more important, books have been completed.

MUSIC DICTIONARY.

Musical terms are gradually introduced throughout the Schaum method books. All eight levels of *Making Music at the Piano* have a short built-in dictionary in the back of each book, featuring the new musical terms which have been presented.

Schaum's *DICTIONARY of MUSICAL TERMS*, with over 1500 words, is a more complete listing with self-pronouncing phonetic syllables. It includes often-used Italian, French, and German words and is designed especially for keyboard students to use from grade school through high school.

Effective Use of
SHEET MUSIC

All teachers realize the value of pupil motivation. For a student, there is great satisfaction and pleasure in the completion of a musical unit, such as a book or piece of sheet music. Likewise, it's an important event when he/she receives a new unit of music. New materials help refresh a student's interest and stimulate his/her musical achievements.

Sheet music is especially effective in boosting a student's musical morale. Because it is a short unit, usually just two to four pages, sheet music is something that can be finished in just a few weeks. Thus, in a rather short time, the pupil can have the thrill of getting a new piece, as well as the satisfaction of completing an entire musical unit. Many teachers like to assign sheet music on a regular basis – such as once every four or five weeks.

Whenever possible, let the student have a voice in the selection of sheet music. For example, offer two or three pieces, at the same level, that you think will interest the individual. Allow him/her to look them over briefly; however, let the pupil make the final choice. When the student makes the selection, there is almost always greater enthusiasm and interest in the music.

It is important to select sheet music that meets both the technical and emotional needs of the pupil. Age, sex, maturity, ability, personality and special interests should all be taken into consideration. The *Schaum Teachers Guide* contains a classified index which you will find very helpful in the selection process. Also included are thematics of select titles. A complete showing of Schaum sheet music thematics is found in the Schaum *Syllabus for Sheet Music*, available free to piano teachers upon request. (Call toll free 800-786-5023.)

CHAPTER 26

WHERE to OBTAIN MUSIC

If you are not familiar with music stores in your area, look in the yellow pages. Larger cities may have the listing, "Music, Sheet." Also look under "Musical Instruments, Dealers," "Organs," or "Pianos." The name of a store can be misleading. "Music Center," "Music Box" or "Music World" could be almost anything. Sometimes the information in the yellow pages display ad can be unclear or incomplete. If your yellow pages do not list any music stores in these categories, skip to the middle of page 86.

You'll discover that some stores handle only guitars and amplifiers. Some handle only records, cassette tapes and stereos. Some sell pianos and organs but have little or no teaching materials. Others carry only pop albums and pop sheet music.

To save time, telephone each of the stores in advance. Even if it's a long distance call, it will be cheaper and faster than making a trip and being disappointed. When you call, get this information about each store:

1. Ask if the store handles keyboard teaching materials. Try to get some idea of the amount and variety of music in stock. Are teachers permitted to browse through the stock? How is the stock organized – by composer, by level, by publisher?

2. If the store does *not* handle teaching materials, ask them to recommend a dealer that does. Be sure to write down the name and location of the other store. Get the phone number, if possible.

3. Find out if the store has a separate person in charge of sheet music and that person's name. What times and days does the sheet music manager work?

4. Ask the store hours. Are they open any evenings? What about Saturday and Sunday?

5. Find out if the store accepts telephone orders or mail orders and will send music out to your home. Are there extra charges for handling, postage or delivery?

6. Does the store have a toll free telephone number? If so, write it down.

7. Does the store give discounts to keyboard teachers? Is there a minimum quantity required for the discount? Is it necessary to pay cash to get the discount?

8. Can you use MasterCard, Visa or Discover Card? Can you establish a store charge account?

9. Get directions to find the store, especially if it is in an unfamiliar section of the city or in another town.

It is definitely worthwhile to shop around. After you have narrowed the choice by telephone, plan to visit the stores that seem to have the largest selection of keyboard teaching music in stock or can quickly deliver what you need. Generally, a store with a separate person in charge of sheet music can provide better service. If mail order service is available, you may want to visit stores in nearby cities or towns.

When looking, it is important that you choose a day when you have plenty of time. You may have to visit several stores, and will need time to familiarize yourself with the one that seems best. Later, when your schedule becomes fuller, this initial time in the store will have been well spent!

Even if you are just starting, don't hesitate to tell the clerk that you are a teacher. Your patronage will be welcome and your questions concerning their inventory and ability to fill orders will be gladly answered.

While at the store, ask the clerk to show you how their keyboard teaching music is organized. Most stores have browser bins, shelves, or file cabinets for use by teachers. Music may be grouped by instrument, publisher, composer or level. SCHAUM music, handled by nearly every store, has been used by successful teachers for many years. The Schaum teaching catalog offers the widest choice of music by any single composer. Schaum continues to offer new and exciting material to make your teaching, and your student's learning, much more enjoyable. Some stores have a special display box featuring the latest Schaum music.

Many stores have a small studio where you may try out new music. If the studio is occupied, you might ask if you could use one of the display pianos or organs on the floor. Some stores put a sign, "please do not touch" or "please do not play" on their new instruments. This is done because of children and inconsiderate adults who might abuse the instrument. If the store knows you are a teacher, there is usually no objection.

If your yellow pages do not list any music stores, it is unlikely that there are any sheet music dealers within 20 or 30 miles. Look up the listing, "Stereo" or "Stereophonic" in the yellow pages. Although these stores are not likely to handle printed music, they may be able to give you the name of a store that does. Be sure to write down the store name, its location and phone number, if possible. Church musicians and public school music teachers will also know the names of stores that handle printed music.

Although it seems reasonable to expect the fastest service from the closest store, this is not always true. It depends on the amount of music the dealer keeps in stock, how efficiently mail or phone orders are handled and how quickly out-of -stock items can be obtained. Don't be afraid of dealers several hundred miles away or even out of state. There are many good mail-order dealers who will send music to all parts of the country. Many of them have toll free telephone numbers for placing orders. You may get better service from a store 300 miles away than one that is 30 miles away. Sometimes a good out-of-state dealer can provide better service than a local store.

For placing mail orders, you should have your own copy of a publisher's catalog such as the *Schaum Teachers Guide*. It enables you to preview the music you are ordering and to survey the entire range of keyboard teaching materials available. If you are unable to obtain a copy from a dealer, you may write directly to the address shown at the end of this chapter.

Of course, the cost of all music which you obtain for lessons should be billed to the student or his/her parents, including all sales taxes which you must pay. See Chapter 9, Section G, "Do You Obtain Music for Your Students?" and Chapter 13, Section E, "Payment of Lesson Fees and Music" for additional information.

Should you need help in locating a reliable mail-order dealer in your part of the country or if you are unable to get satisfactory service from your current dealer, you may write directly to:

Schaum Publications, Inc.
10235 N. Port Washington Rd.
Mequon, WI 53092

LESSON PLANNING

CHAPTER 27

FIRST LESSON

The significance of the first lesson cannot be overemphasized. Initial attitudes, expectations, and relationships will have a lasting effect. You hope to establish a friendly rapport with your students so that they will radiate your own enthusiasm. Let's go through the steps of creating a successful first lesson.

PRIOR to the FIRST LESSON.

Your first contact with the parent of a prospective student is an opportunity to gather information. This can be done on the telephone without taking time during the lesson. Mother's and father's names and occupations, address, phone number, age of student, grade in school, music study in school (another instrument), previous lessons (music, ballet, acrobatics, gymnastics, etc.) can be conveniently placed on the "History and Record Sheet" in the Schaum *Music Teacher's Organizer.*

ESSENTIAL HABITS to ESTABLISH.

Many important habits and attitudes are formed at the first lesson and during the first month's study. Chapter 13 provides helpful insights and information.

ADVICE for HANDLING NEW STUDENTS.

The first lesson will be very satisfying to a beginner who is able to learn at least one or two pieces, even though the music is very simple. There is a lot to be covered at this first lesson. You may be tempted to make detailed explanations that really don't help the pupil learn the first piece and may be confusing or overwhelming. Don't talk too much! Keep explanations at a minimum — just what is essential to learning the first pieces of music. *Let the pupil get a lot of keyboard experience.*

BEGINNING the FIRST LESSON.

Ask the student to play something for you. You may just get a muddled melody or a few awkward chords. Be encouraging, as this will help dispel any inhibitions right from the start, make the student feel important, and may reveal a musical ear. If a shy child refuses to play, don't insist; the student must feel comfortable in what he/she is doing.

Now is the time to establish good posture and seating position. Then proceed to acquaint the student with the keyboard, black key groups, the location of middle C, and how the seven letters of the musical alphabet repeat over and over.

Use your imagination in creating a picture to dramatize the location of each letter at the keyboard. For example, C is located at the bottom of the two black keys, as if sliding down a hill on a sled. D, the "sandwich note," is like the peanut butter between two slices of bread. These descriptions will make lasting impressions and make learning fun.

Proper hand positions, with fingers curved, should be illustrated by showing the student how to make a tunnel over five white keys. You can pass a pencil through this tunnel, pretending it is a train. This will help teach the concept that only the *fingertips* should touch the keys.

PREPARING to READ MUSIC.

Schaum's *Making Music at the Piano, Primer Level* is one of the most exciting books available for the child beginner. It is recommended that the student's first encounter at the keyboard use the "Keyboard Touch Finder," which is included with the book. This starts developing the sense of touch from the outset. It fosters the important habit of keeping eyes on the music and prevents looking down at the hands and keyboard. The "Touch Finder" is illustrated on page 64.

FIRST PIECES.

Along with the first two "Blind Flying Drills," most students should be able to start the first two or three pieces in *Making Music at the Piano, Primer Level.* The first three pieces use only middle C with both hands.

PARENT PARTICIPATION.

If the new student is a grade-schooler, it is wise to ask one of the parents to come along and sit through at least the first lesson. This way you can establish practice rules, discuss questions, and make clear your expectations for regular attendance, lesson payments, missed lessons, etc. See Chapter 15, "Parents' Role."

IMPORTANCE of WRITTEN ASSIGNMENTS.

New students need considerable guidance to form good practice habits. For the sake of both parent and child, it is essential that you provide a written list of what is to be practiced. A handy and practical assignment book is the *Progressive Practice Plans,* published by Schaum Publications, Inc. One page is devoted to each week's assignment. Space is provided for you to specify the number of times per day that you want each piece practiced. A sample page is shown below.

Date: _____	Assigned Times Per Day	WRITE IN NUMBER OF TIMES EACH PIECE IS PLAYED							Grade or Comments
Title or Page		MON	TUE	WED	THU	FRI	SAT	SUN	
TOTAL TIME PRACTICED →									

Sample page from *Progressive Practice Plans.*

ENDING the LESSON.

The ideal way to end the first lesson is for you to play a showy piece to impress both student and parent. This is especially important when you are first starting because it adds credibility to your teaching.

CHAPTER 28

HOW MUCH to ASSIGN at EACH LESSON?

As explained in Chapter 16, "Curriculum Development," most lessons will consist of assignments from four different books:

1. Method Book
2. Theory Book
3. Technic Book
4. Repertoire Book

Usually, you will assign at least one page from each of these four books every week. In addition, it is desirable to include some review work and memory work on a regular basis. For example, some teachers have their students memorize at least one piece every month. (See Chapter 31, "Review Work," and Chapter 32, "Memorizing.") For variety, sheet music should often be substituted for pieces in the repertoire book.

Ideally, you will want to assign sufficient material to challenge the student but not to overwhelm him. You will also want to tailor the length of each week's assignment so that you can reasonably expect to hear everything at the next lesson. There will not always be an equal amount of material assigned in each of the four curriculum categories every week. You will not always assign the same quantity of work to the same student every week.

Obviously, there will be differences in the work assigned to bright, average, and slow students. There will also be differences according to the student's age, maturity, and personality. This clearly is an important advantage of private lessons. Bright students will need to be challenged, usually with longer assignments, more review and memory work, and with optional extra work such as transposing and cross-hand playing, as encountered in the method books. You can be a little more particular and more demanding with bright students than with others. However, it's important to consider age, maturity, and personality in the approach that is taken to each individual. A bright student who is very sensitive to criticism needs to be handled differently than a bright student who is overconfident. For additional advice, see Chapter 5, "Psychology of Teaching."

Younger and less mature students should generally have shorter assignments than those who are older. This is because younger students have shorter concentration spans and usually cannot be expected to practice as much. You may find a surprisingly mature 10-year old who can be expected to accomplish more than an immature 12-year old. Adults can generally be given longer assignments than children, although you also have to consider how "busy" the adult is with other work and activities.

The musical level will also affect the number of pages and pieces assigned. Primer Level, Level One, and Level Two pieces are quite short, therefore two or three pieces from the method book, plus one or two theory pages, one or two technic pieces, and one or two repertoire pieces would be a typical assignment at these levels for the average student. A bright student could be expected to do a little more. As the music becomes longer, more difficult, and requires more practice, the number of pages and pieces assigned each week will gradually decrease.

The work schedule of the individual student should also be considered. As pupils get older and become more involved in extra-curricular activities, sports, scouts, etc., and have more homework, you may have to adjust the lesson assignment. There will also be special events such as school plays, term papers, and field trips that will affect the time available for practice. Students should be encouraged to let you know in advance when conflicting events will interfere with practice time.

Variations in mood, especially during adolescence, should influence what and how much you decide to assign. A student who is optimistic and cheerful can be given a longer assignment with more new materials. Another time, if the same pupil is moody or discouraged, a shorter assignment or an assignment with easier work may be better. Your choice of new and review materials will affect how much and how difficult the practice will be. Chapter 5, "Psychology of Teaching," offers additional insights.

But, Mrs. Higgins,
my Aunt Joan never plays it that way!

CHAPTER 29

HOW to FIT EVERYTHING into a 30 MINUTE LESSON

It is best to hear everything you have assigned *every week*. The most important reason is that mistakes and misunderstandings that have developed between lessons are otherwise practiced for another week and become more engrained and harder to correct. Students who have practiced conscientiously look forward to getting recognition and praise for their efforts. They are disappointed if you are not able to hear their accomplishments each week. Bright but lazy students soon discover that they can evade work if it's not likely that their lack of practice will be discovered.

Teachers often ask, how do you find time to cover assignments in a method book, and also fit theory, technic, repertoire, review, and memorizing into a 30-minute lesson? Here are some ideas that will help.

WRITTEN PRACTICE ASSIGNMENTS.

The single piece of advice that is most helpful is to *write down the entire lesson assignment on ONE page or sheet*. This will be a simple list showing the page numbers or titles of pieces assigned in each book. Use abbreviations that both you and the student will understand. It is logical to organize it by units of the Four-Book Plan: Method, Theory, Technic, and Repertoire. A sample assignment page might look like this:

Method: p. 12 and 13;   Review p. 9

Theory: Less. 8

Technic: No. 7 and 8;   Review No. 6

Repertoire: p. 17;   Memorize p. 12

Obviously, this assignment page is not to take the place of the special notations, corrections, and reminders which you write on the individual pages of music. In addition to the assignment page, many teachers also like to write the starting date on each page of music.

Specialized assignment books are described in Chapter 14, "Practice Habits for Students." For more advanced students, you could simply use a small lined spiral notebook, devoting one page to each week's lesson. Another idea is to write the assignment on a piece of paper which you staple onto the front of one of the books.

These written assignments help in several ways. They remind the student what needs to be done. They show parents what is expected during practice. When you have twenty or more students each week, it helps you to remember exactly what has been assigned to each student. But most importantly, written assignments help you organize the time devoted to each lesson. As soon as the student arrives, ask for the assignment book and look over the current page. This gives you an opportunity to see what needs to be covered and to organize in your mind how much time to allot to each part of the assignment.

MOVE QUICKLY from ONE PART of the ASSIGNMENT to the NEXT.

The written assignment page will help you decide what comes next. You don't always have to start at the top of the assignment list and take everything in sequence. For variety, you may skip around or start from the bottom of the list. This keeps students on their toes. Be very businesslike and efficient. If you should finish everything before the end of the lesson time, take the opportunity for additional review, memory work, ensemble playing, ear training, etc.

Obviously, this will require self-discipline and special effort for you but it is well worthwhile. After working with several different students for three or four weeks it will become easier. Eventually, when this lesson planning becomes automatic, it will be a great asset to your teaching efficiency.

At first, you will probably discover that some of your lesson assignments are too long and cannot fit into a 30-minute time period. You will then have to shorten the assignment for the next week and perhaps make adjustments in future assignments. As you get more experience, you should gradually improve your ability to keep within the scheduled lesson time.

AVOID UNNECESSARY TALKING.

Usually the student gains more by playing than by conversation. Keep explanations short. Consider the age, maturity, and musical level of each student and try to limit talking to just the essentials. Elaborate explanations not only consume valuable time, but may be confusing or boring, especially to a young student. As mentioned in Chapter 36, "Adults," there are times that a little gossip helps put the student at ease. However, be very careful; this chit-chat can easily get out of hand and take more time than is beneficial. Clever but lazy students sometimes use talking as a way of avoiding the lesson when they are not prepared.

MINIMIZE the TIME TAKEN
with SEALS or STARS.

As suggested in Chapter 33, "Motivation and Awards," you will probably be giving award seals or colored stars to children as they successfully complete each unit of work. Although it takes experience and self-discipline, try to make up your mind quickly on the seal or star to give. Have them handy so they can be given without delay. The time taken by the pupil to paste on the seal is an opportunity for you to plan the next portion of the lesson.

AVOID INTERRUPTIONS.

It is the teacher's responsibility to minimize outside interruptions during lessons. Several ideas have been presented in Chapter 8, "Schedule Organizing," and in Chapter 10, "Studio Layout."

The most common distractions are the telephone and doorbell. If possible, have someone else attend to them while you are teaching. If you can afford it, you might consider a telephone answering machine to use during the times you teach. If you have to answer the phone, explain that you are teaching and that you will call back later. Make it as brief as possible.

Although your goal should be to *hear everything that you have assigned at each lesson,* it is not always possible to do this. No matter how carefully you have planned, unexpected things arise. Often, it may simply be that the pupil arrives late. Extra time is sometimes needed to explain one concept or aspect of technic. This means that unfinished parts of the lesson must be delayed until the following week. In most cases it is best to keep the regular 30-minute lesson and NOT give extra time. If you run late, it is unfair to other students that follow on your schedule. If you frequently give extra lesson time, it will soon become something the student takes for granted.

As your students advance into Level Five and beyond, you should consider scheduling a longer lesson with a proportionate increase in your lesson fee. Very talented pupils who are able to absorb longer assignments may also benefit from a longer lesson. Many teachers have found 40 or 45 minutes to be a practical length for these circumstances. Students in Level Seven need a full hour lesson because the pieces are longer and more complicated.

INTEGRATING MUSIC APPRECIATION.
Music appreciation can be taught as part of a regular lesson without taking extra time. Schaum method books include many elements of music appreciation. Supplementary repertoire books offer opportunities for more detailed information. For example, at Level 1 the student is ready for one of the following Schaum "Classic Melodies" books:

Great Ballets	*Great Operas*
Great Composers	*Great Symphonies*

The following repertoire books are especially designed for music appreciation:

Classic Themes, Book 1 . . . . Level 2
Classic Themes, Book 2 . . . . Level 3

CHAPTER 30

HOW LONG to WORK on the SAME PIECE?

Generally, it is recommended that students in the early levels of music, Primer Level through Level Four, spend not more than three successive weeks on the same piece. By this time, the pupil has usually reached a plateau in his/her progress and is getting sick and tired of practicing the same piece. You're probably tired of listening to it too.

If you can't conscientiously give a "satisfactory" award seal after three weeks, discontinue work on the piece and tell the student, "We'll come back to this later." In most cases, after a lapse of three to four weeks' time, the pupil can go back to the same piece with a fresh outlook and complete it with little difficulty.

Students in intermediate and advanced levels (Level 5 and up) have longer and more complicated pieces which often require more than three weeks' work. Keep in mind, most adults and teens have sufficient maturity to work more than three weeks on the same piece, regardless of level.

STANDARDS of MUSICIANSHIP

When deciding how long to work on the same piece, you must also determine the standards of musicianship and performance to be upheld. This requires an individual decision for each student. Age, maturity, personality, talent and musical level all must be considered.

Your purpose, as a teacher, is to help each student make the most of his/her own musical potential. But it's difficult to know when and how much to push a student. You want each one to be successful at the keyboard and also to really enjoy the music. To do this it's best to step back and get some perspective. Look beyond the week to week progress and judge what has happened during a period of six months or more. Consult Chapter 2, "Outlook Toward Teaching," and Chapter 5, "Psychology of Teaching."

CHAPTER 31

REVIEW WORK

A typical student will work one, two or sometimes three weeks before finishing a piece of music. During that time, most practice effort is devoted to the basics – correct notes, rhythm, fingering, dynamics, etc. Although you give an award seal or star when a piece is completed, there are often things that the student could have done better. Review is an opportunity to improve and work on the fine points of performance. It's a good idea to have one or two review pieces as part of every week's assignment.

A grading system for each piece, using different award seals or colored stars, will help you to pick out pieces for the student to review. (See Chapter 33, "Motivation and Awards.") Those that were satisfactory or good are the most likely candidates. Wait two or three weeks before starting the review. This gives the student a rest from practicing the same piece.

There must always be a purpose for review. Tell the pupil what needs to be improved. Accuracy of rhythm, notes, fingering, dynamics, phrasing and pedaling are elements that often need extra work.

What about pieces rated very good or excellent? These may be memorized to add a challenge to the review. Maybe the tempos could be a bit faster. Certainly they should be played without any hesitation in the flow of rhythm.

REPERTOIRE.
Review pieces should be used to build a repertoire. Each student should master five or six pieces that can be played with confidence and polish, preferably memorized. This repertoire may change frequently, with newer pieces replacing older ones. Such pieces could be played at home when company comes or relatives visit. When it's time for a recital, you and the student can choose the best from among present or former repertoire pieces.

CHAPTER 32

MEMORIZING

Playing from memory is an important part of musicianship which adds considerably to self-confidence. The discipline and experience of memorizing music is valuable when memory work is required for public speaking, poetry, drama, or vocal music.

Ability to memorize is an aptitude which varies from one person to another. It comes very easily to some and is a struggle for others. The primary goal is to play fluently and musically. Memorizing is to be encouraged but not to the point of causing frustration and despair.

Memorizing should be part of review work that is started shortly after lessons begin. Memory work should be a regular part of a student's curriculum. It is advisable to assign one piece to be memorized at least every three to four weeks. Memorized pieces should be part of the student's repertoire. In this way, memorizing becomes almost routine and usually presents no problem as the student goes on to more advanced levels of music. It is a considerable advantage when preparing for a recital.

Transfer students, who have not been trained in memory work as beginners, may have difficulties. Their memory training will start with very short, easy pieces — at least two levels below their music reading level. A special supplementary book could be chosen for this purpose. Let memory work be a part of almost every lesson. Gradually increase the length and difficulty of the memory work, until it reaches the level of their current method book.

CHAPTER 33

MOTIVATION and AWARDS

Sincere praise is one of the easiest rewards to give and costs nothing. You can begin at the first lesson by saying something complimentary about the student. For girls it might be a pretty blouse, shoes or hair style; for boys, Nike or Reebok (athletic shoes), belt, jeans or shirt. Right away, you have made that person feel good about themselves and more receptive to what you will be teaching. At succeeding lessons, praise the student for things that are done right – if only for having clean hands or keeping feet flat on the floor.

Use praise judiciously. Most people are quick to see through a fake compliment; however, heartfelt praise can be very meaningful. In addition, a system of rewards is very effective for motivation.

AWARD SEALS and STARS.

Each piece and workbook page should get an award seal or star when satisfactorily completed. Schaum's *Musical Award Seals* and *Special Merit Award Seals* can be the basis of a structured system. Various picture seals can be used for "satisfactory" work. Other seals are labeled "good," "very good," "excellent" and "special merit." "Special merit" should be reserved only for an outstanding and nearly perfect performance.

Instead of award seals, you can use different color stars, for example, gold = superior, silver = excellent, blue = very good, green = good, red = satisfactory.

Try to be consistent in the standard of performance needed for each star or sticker. If you are easy-going one day and more fussy the next time, the awards lose their meaning and value.

The "Report Sheet" of Schaum's *Music Teacher Organizer* provides space for a star to grade the overall lesson. After a certain number of starred lessons, the student receives a small gift. The gifts could be something homemade, a small music boutique item, or a certificate.

CERTIFICATES.

Completion of a book is an important event that deserves special recognition for the pupil. Each book of Schaum's *Making Music at the Piano* method has a "Certificate of Progress" at the end. Schaum also publishes two sizes of general purpose certificates which can be used for books without built-in certificates.

Music Award Certificate
(size 5 x 7 inches)

Certificate of Musical Achievement
(size: 8 x 10 inches)

Certificates can also be used for:

Completion of "Four Book Plan" at one level

Recital participation

Contest or audition participation

Completion of a special musical project such as a sonata or a concerto movement

Participation in the fifth or tenth recital

Perfect attendance for one semester

These certificates can be given variety and greater significance by use of Schaum's *GOLD AWARD SEALS*. The gold seal should be reserved for more important achievements. For major accomplishments, add a narrow piece (approx. ¼ inch wide) of colored ribbon about four to five inches long. The ribbon should be folded over to form an upside-down V-shape. Attach the ribbon to the certificate by placing the gold seal over the fold in the ribbon. For example, for completion of the "Four Book Plan" at the primer level, use *red* ribbon to correspond with the color used for the books at this level.

MUSIC BOUTIQUE ITEMS.

Major awards may be chosen from various musical stationery, buttons, statuettes, plaques, jewelry, and clothing. Give careful thought to the cost of the gift as related to the accomplishment being rewarded.

PERFORMANCES.

Most students are motivated by opportunities to show off their keyboard accomplishments. You should encourage and help create occasions for them to perform. Start modestly, with a very small audience. Performances may be for:

1. A small group of your other students.

2. Grandparents or other relatives.

3. The school classroom or Sunday school.

4. School and community talent shows and variety shows.

5. Part of a religious service.

6. Contests, festivals, and auditions sponsored by local, county, or state musical organizations.

7. A choir, chorus, or soloist (as accompanist).

8. School band or orchestra (as a soloist).

Always confer with parents to schedule and prepare for these occasions. For additional information see Chapter 31, "Review Work," Chapter 32, "Memorizing," Chapter 42, "Recitals," and Chapter 41, "Contests and Auditions."

HANDLING
SPECIAL SITUATIONS

CHAPTER 34

AGES 4 - 5 - 6

Most teachers agree that there are great differences in the learning readiness of students, especially at age 4, 5, and 6. Attention span, attitude, degree of maturity, physical development, and muscular coordination of eyes and fingers all affect the rate of progress at a keyboard instrument. Because of these limitations, not all children of this age are ready for lessons; however, for too long we have underestimated their learning capacity. Although they cannot be expected to learn as quickly as an older child, a surprising number of these youngsters of 4, 5, and 6 can be taught successfully.

This is a delightful age — they are loving and respectful; their minds are fresh and alert. Above all, teaching these young children requires a "heaping cup of patience." You must be able to cope with very short attention spans (two to five minutes) and be prepared to change quickly from one activity to another during the lesson. You may want to schedule a lesson of just 20 minutes rather than a full 30 minutes.

Most teachers have been approached by parents of a 4, 5, or 6 year old who are eager for their youngster to begin lessons. They proudly tell how their child has exhibited great interest and enthusiasm and perhaps has been able to pick out short melodies at the keyboard. The parents seem convinced that they have a budding Mozart. This child is certainly a good prospect for keyboard lessons!

The best way to start a pupil of 4, 5, or 6 is for a trial period of two or three months. The parents should understand that it will take this amount of time to adequately evaluate their child's learning readiness. The only prerequisites are that the child knows the first seven letters of the alphabet, can count to five, and has enough finger dexterity to play the keys one at a time. The Schaum *KEYBOARD TALENT HUNT, Book 1* is a method designed especially for this age. The child learns music by reading letter names instead of notes. Nursery rhyme melodies and illustrations are provided. The student also learns finger numbers and gains basic five-finger dexterity in both hands. As a companion, the Schaum *KEYBOARD ALPHABET WORK-BOOK* is recommended.

Depending upon the proficiency shown by the child during the trial period, there will be two options. If things are going well, you should continue the work in *Keyboard Talent Hunt, Book 1,* and *Keyboard Alphabet Workbook.* However, if the pupil has difficulty in these books it does not necessarily mean there is a lack of musical potential or talent. It simply indicates that the child has probably started lessons too early and that his *musical learning readiness is not sufficiently developed.* In such cases, it is advisable to stop lessons temporarily, with the understanding that study be resumed after waiting for at least six to twelve months.

It is advisable to finish most of the workbook pages at the lesson, especially when a new concept is presented or when there is trouble retaining an old concept. Obviously, children will not be able to read the instructions, therefore it is important that the assignment be understood before leaving the studio.

Pupils at this age vary widely in their learning rates and amount of retention. It is quite normal for very young children to forget (partially or completely) what they have been taught from one week to the next. The ability to remember is something that develops gradually and differs from one child to another. For this reason much repetition and review are included in the *Keyboard Alphabet Workbook*. In some cases, you may need to provide additional help until the learning concepts are firmly in mind.

When *Keyboard Talent Hunt, Book 1* has been completed there are two ways to proceed.

1. If additional work with letter-name melodies is needed, use *Keyboard Talent Hunt, Book 2*. This provides the added experience of reading and playing with both hands together. Very simple accompaniments in the left hand are added to right hand melodies.

2. Many students will be ready to begin traditional note reading and may proceed to a child beginner method using the Middle-C approach such as Schaum's *Making Music at the Piano, Primer Level*. These very young students often need to be kept at the Primer Level longer than an older child. There is an ample choice of Primer Level supplements in the *Schaum Piano Teachers Guide*.

You may also want to organize small classes of these youngsters. The book, *Keyboard Classes for Age Four to Seven,* contains complete instructions plus detailed lesson plans for two semesters of work. See Chapter 39, "Class Teaching," for more details.

CHAPTER 35

TEENAGERS

CLUES to ADOLESCENCE.

The start of adolescence varies widely from one person to another. Generally, it starts sooner in girls than boys. Be on the lookout as early as age 11 or 12 for individuals who seem quite mature – either mentally or physically. Be aware that adolescence is a time of swings in mood and personality with many ups and downs. A person who is adult-like one day may be childish or silly the next day. An individual who is quite serious about computers or chemistry may still sleep with a teddy bear.

WORKING SUCCESSFULLY with TEENS.

As with adults, teens need great patience and empathy for their feelings. Although teens are in the process of becoming more assertive and opinionated, they also are more self-conscious and sensitive than children. Be prepared to handle unexpected changes of mood from one lesson to the next.

Maintaining a steady, optimistic outlook is important. As with students of any age, beware of those who are lazy. Teens are quite imaginative in fabricating excuses for lack of progress. As was discussed in Chapter 5, "Psychology of Teaching," be genuine and sincere in your outlook. At times, this may mean being genuinely disappointed or even angry. As with adults, spending a little time just talking during each lesson is often good psychology.

A MUSICAL COMPROMISE.

Style of music is often a problem with teenagers. Peer pressure and music heard relentlessly on radio and TV influence their preference, which is usually quite different from your own. Although you hope to instill a sense of musical value and a taste for the great composers, it is sometimes a losing battle!

Teens like pop music; maybe you don't. But, if you limit their diet to serious music, most teens will become turned off. A compromise is necessary. It is far better to assign a mix of musical styles, including all kinds of pop music, and keep the teen active at the keyboard, than to insist on unpalatable music and force an eventual end to lessons.

As an educator, you should recognize that all styles of music including jazz, blues, boogie, swing, ragtime, etc. have something of value worth teaching, whether or not their sound appeals to you. Often, the rhythms are tricky and make excellent syncopation studies. There is also value in studying the technical and harmonic aspects of pop music.

Along with pop music, assign at least one or two pieces in a method book each week to continue some contact with serious music. Also, continue some theory work. You've got to hang in there! It may be a long wait before teens eventually recognize that serious music has something to offer. In the meantime, their note reading, rhythmic and technical skills will be improving.

The Schaum catalog offers a good variety of pop style music that is convenient and attractive. Included are:

Easy Boogie, Books 1-2
Easy Ragtime for Level 3
Jazz Jamboree
Rhythm & Blues, Books 1-2-3
Scott Joplin, Ragtime Rage, Books 1-2

CHORDS and IMPROVISING

Teens and many adults like to do their own thing. Chords and improvising offer an opportunity to do something creative with music. The Schaum *Easy Keyboard Harmony* books teach improvising and accompaniment from standard chord symbols. The advanced books of *Easy Keyboard Harmony* also teach melody improvising and fill-ins. See Chapter 40, "Improvising and Chord Symbols." The *Schaum Teachers Guide* has a large selection of albums and sheet music solos with chord symbols.

CHAPTER 36
ADULTS

WHY ADULTS TAKE LESSONS.

There is a growing interest in keyboard study among adults. Parents, whose children are off to school or have left home, need music as a new interest to offset their "empty nest syndrome." Retired individuals want to pursue the keyboard as a hobby — "something they've always wanted to do." Adults also take lessons to fulfill social needs. They enjoy your companionship during the lesson as much as the music itself.

JOYS of TEACHING ADULTS.

Adults are mature, cooperative, and have better powers of concentration than children. There are no discipline problems! They're fun to talk to. They study because they *want* to, not because of parental pressure. Working with adults can enrich your life as much as it does theirs.

There's also a simple psychology here. Because adults are *paying* for their own lessons, they usually are quite conscientious and try to get their money's worth.

ADULT MISCONCEPTIONS.

Adults are often impatient. They think that simply being "grown up" should enable them to learn music ten times faster than a child. Perhaps an overzealous instrument salesman baited them with the false idea of becoming an instant virtuoso. Maybe they never fully understood the extent of training and study needed to play a musical instrument.

A few adults set rather high hopes for themselves which are ambitious fantasies rather than realistic goals. Your challenge as a teacher will be to gently bring their ambitions down to earth.

Realistically, adults need to learn the same music fundamentals at about the same pace as a child. Unfortunately, many adults have more of a struggle developing the necessary coordination and muscle control.

FRAGILE MUSICAL EGO — HANDLE WITH CARE.

Starting lessons as an adult can be a humbling experience, especially with many mistaken ideas about learning the keyboard. The relationship between the adult student and teacher is not the same as it is for a child. Children, for the most part, accept criticism and corrections matter-of-factly. Adults, however, see you as their *peer*. They are often very self-conscious and are much more likely to take criticism personally.

You need to be ever so gentle in pointing out an adult's mistakes. They are sometimes utterly crushed when you find so many things wrong with a piece after they have worked diligently all week.

Insecurity and nervousness are quite common. You may often hear a frustrated adult say, "...but this piece was *perfect* when I played it at home." (It probably was!) Adults may need more patient encouragement and coddling than a child.

Try everything you know to help put the adult at ease. Remember, they are often seeking companionship along with music; therefore, it is not a waste of time to spend the first four or five minutes of a lesson in pure gossip if it helps make the adult more relaxed.

Take a sympathetic attitude. Imagine how you would feel taking private bassoon lessons — certainly no easy task! For an adult, it takes a lot of courage to pursue private lessons. It's often reassuring to say how much you admire them for taking the time and expense needed for music lessons.

TEACHING MATERIALS for ADULTS.

Obviously, children's books designed with juvenile titles, silly verses, and cartoon illustrations are unsuitable and even demeaning for an adult. Although they need to learn the same nitty-gritty of notes, rhythms, fingering, etc., adults need a mature approach. They also expect more sophisticated music. Schaum's *PIANO for ADULTS, Beginner Level* is designed for mature tastes and features music appreciation.

Adults should have the same "Four-Book Plan" curriculum as that recommended for children. See Chapter 24, "Use of Supplements."

Is it O.K. if I stand for my lesson today?
These jeans are new
and I haven't broken them in yet.

CHAPTER 37

TRANSFER STUDENTS

You may receive calls from students that are *not* beginners. Some will have moved from another community; others are not happy with their current teacher. Adults often have had lessons before, but have been away from the keyboard for a number of years. Though it may be a little while before you feel comfortable in accepting such students, these guidelines will help.

As with beginners, get the routine information for your records. Include the name of the previous teacher(s), when, and how long the students studied. If they are changing teachers, it is important to find out the *reason* why.

FIRST LESSON WITH YOU.
Ask transfer students to bring old music from their last year of study. If they have forgotten what it was, have them bring all of their old music. Listen carefully as they play two or three old pieces. Also, ask them to sight read some new pieces which you select from different levels of Schaum's *Making Music at the Piano* books. If in doubt, start with the preparatory level. Have students read a piece near the beginning. If there is no hesitation, skip ahead quickly and have them read a piece from the middle of the book. Again, if there is no trouble, skip ahead and read a piece near the end of the book. Continue this procedure with each successive level until you reach the point where they can no longer sight read fluently. This will serve as a guide in deciding where to resume study. If you are in doubt, assign a method book one level easier.

USE of OLD MUSIC.
Psychologically, it is best for the student to make a fresh start with new music, especially when there has been dissatisfaction with a previous teacher. If the student is insistent, or cannot afford new music, you might finish the old books and then convert to appropriate material in the Schaum system. However, this is possible only if the level of the old music is not too difficult.

If you feel strongly that the old music is inferior or too difficult, do not hesitate to say so. After all, *you* are the teacher and must be the final judge of what materials are appropriate! A tactful way of avoiding the use of old books is to tell the student, "We'll come back to them later."

RESUMING AFTER a PERIOD of ABSENCE from the KEYBOARD.

These students may not be able to play *any* old pieces and may have difficulty sight reading even at the preparatory level. You will, of course, have to start them in a beginner's book. Since this may be somewhat embarrassing or discouraging, especially for adults, you should assure them that their progress will be faster than if they've had no previous lessons. As lessons proceed, they will probably discover many concepts that they remember either partially or completely. During this time you will need special patience and should give lots of encouragement – even for a little progress.

PREVIOUS STUDY of ANOTHER INSTRUMENT.

Students who have played a band or orchestra instrument will know rhythms, dynamics, phrasing and tempos, but their note reading will probably be limited to one clef. If they have played a treble clef instrument, emphasis will have to be given to reading bass clef notes and vice versa. All such students will need development of finger dexterity at the keyboard. They should be started at the beginner's level.

RECOMMENDED LIBRARY for STUDENT EVALUATION.

When you decide to accept transfer students, you should have at least the first five levels of Schaum's *Making Music at the Piano* books on hand for sight reading. This includes Primer Level, plus Levels 1-2-3-4. If your budget does not permit such an expenditure, perhaps you could obtain them on approval from a music store. The first five levels of the Schaum *Fingerpower* books are also good for sight reading.

CHAPTER 38

GOOD MUSICAL EAR: PROBLEMS and BLESSINGS

A "musical ear" is a gift that is actually a mixture of several musical aptitudes.

1. *Musical memory* is the ability to remember melodies, series of chords, or whole pieces of music. However, it does not necessarily include a sense of rhythm, relative pitch, or perfect pitch.

2. *Sense of rhythm* is the ability to remember and duplicate various rhythms.

3. *Relative pitch* is the ability to recognize musical intervals by listening and thereby to name subsequent pitches after hearing and knowing the identity of the starting pitch.

4. *Perfect pitch,* which is quite unusual, is the ability to identify, using only the sense of hearing, the names of individual musical pitches.

All four of these aptitudes are inborn but occur in varying degrees and combinations. All require development and can be improved with proper training. For example, perfect pitch (sometimes called absolute pitch) can simply be naming or duplicating a single pitch by singing. With further training it can include playing an instrument, and writing down music notes. In some persons, perfect pitch can be developed into naming or duplicating intervals, chords, phrases, and even whole pieces of music. Relative pitch, sense of rhythm, and musical memory can be similarly developed.

Students who have a good musical ear usually learn faster and more easily than those without. This often presents a problem to the teacher, especially if not recognized early. Such students are apt to rely on their ear and be slow in learning to read notes. In some cases, students avoid note reading as much as possible. Obviously, there must be lots of sight reading experience. It is important to remember: *RARELY play a new piece for such students.* Take time at the lesson to watch the sight reading of each new piece. Be sure that it is played with the correct notes, rhythm, and fingering. You may demonstrate portions of the rhythm or notes that need help, but not the entire piece. If necessary, have them play the new piece a second time as you supervise. *Do NOT play the piece for the student until it has been practiced alone at least one week.* It helps to choose as much *unfamiliar* music as possible.

Sometimes you may get a transfer student who plays mostly by ear and reads notes quite poorly. His playing ability is usually far beyond his note reading ability. This is one of the most difficult teaching situations to handle. Before accepting this transfer student, it's best to talk to both student and parents and reach an understanding of how you plan to proceed. You may want to explain that in the past, too much reliance had been placed on the ear, and not enough on note reading skills. Point out the main advantage of note reading — eventual musical independence which is a great asset when participating in musical groups such as a choir, band, or orchestra. Many styles of music can be explored and a higher degree of musicianship can be attained with adequate note reading skills.

Your challenge will be to give remedial work to improve note reading while keeping the student motivated and his ear challenged. First, determine the present note reading level by sight reading from method books, starting at the primer level. You will need to assign lots of music reading at or slightly below this present level. Be sure that it is *unfamiliar* music — to purposely force the pupil to read. A majority of time at each lesson will have to be devoted to sight reading. It is not necessary that each piece be practiced all week and finished. Some can be read through three or four times and others, probably those that have most appeal, assigned for practice between lessons. Because a lot of music is consumed in this process, you may prefer to let the student borrow music you have in your private library rather than requiring the purchase of music that is used only for a short time. As the sight reading improves, the level of music can be advanced. It will be a slow process, but your aim will be to bring the level of note reading near to the level of playing.

You will want to assign a workbook to assist in improving note reading. Those which reinforce written work with keyboard practice, such as the Schaum *Theory Workbooks* and *Keynote Spellers,* are highly recommended. Be sure the workbook pages are *practiced at the keyboard* as recommended in both of these series. This gives additional note reading experience. If necessary, assign more than one workbook at the same level.

Along with this remedial note reading work, you should also explore ways to develop and challenge the ear. These suggestions should be used both for transfer students and for your regular students who have a good ear.

1. Ask the student to play by ear (without notes) an excerpt of a simple familiar tune between four and eight measures long. As an assignment, ask him to write the notes of the melody on manuscript paper. Leave one extra staff blank so that bass notes can be added later. If necessary, give him a keyboard chart that fits behind the black keys. The Schaum *Keyboard Notation Chart* is recommended. Additional assignments can involve gradually longer and more difficult melodies. You can also ask the student to devise a simple accompaniment and write (on the same manuscript paper) either the chord symbols used or the notes for the accompaniment.

2. Have the student transpose a short, familiar melody by ear at the keyboard. Then, have him write the notes for the transposed version on manuscript paper. An accompaniment could be added, as explained in the paragraph above.

3. Occasionally, let the student learn a piece entirely by ear (sometimes called "by rote") — just for fun. It might even be learned from a cassette recording you have made that would be suitable for his level. Have him try to write the melody notes on manuscript paper.

4. When the student has reached at least Level Two, have him start in Schaum's *Easy Keyboard Harmony, Book 1.* This series systematically presents improvising an accompaniment from chord symbols, and learning to write and spell chords correctly. This is an especially good method of developing a good ear. In Books 4 and 5, various ways of melody improvising are presented. See Chapter 40, "Improvising and Chord Symbols."

All four of the suggestions above involve use of manuscript paper. In effect, the student is learning note reading in reverse — by hearing and playing first and then writing the notes. Schaum also offers a *Scale Speller* which presents scale construction and analysis. Similar analysis and construction is used in Schaum's *Arpeggio Speller, Interval Speller,* and *Chord Speller.* All four of these books offer possibilities for more refined ear training.

CHAPTER 39

CLASS TEACHING

Learning the keyboard in a group works best with beginners and in Level One and Level Two. If you have the opportunity, teens or adults may also be taught in classes. Matching abilities and rate of progress is the key to an effective group. If you are willing to do some experimenting, you might form a small class by combining two or three beginners who are close in age. Age matching is important with children, especially at age eight and below. There are great differences in both physical and mental development at these ages.

Class teaching requires careful preparation on your part with lots of planning before each lesson. The same "Four-Book Plan" curriculum recommended for private lessons can also be adapted to classes.

KEYBOARD CLASSES for AGE FOUR to SEVEN, published by Schaum Publications, Inc., is a comprehensive text with lesson plans for two semesters. Even if you have never handled very young children or attempted teaching in a group, this book provides in-depth details of all steps along the way to help organize your first class. Working with preschoolers is like a breath of fresh air because of their appealing innocence and desire to please.

This book forms an acquaintance with musical letter names at the keyboard, establishes the feeling for a steady beat, and begins development of basic five-finger dexterity. It provides a general music background and prepares the child for private lessons on piano or organ. Detailed lesson plans are provided for two semesters. The first semester consists of ten class lessons; the second semester has twelve class lessons. It is preferable that these class semesters coincide with the semesters in the public schools. The suggested duration of each class ranges from 30 to 60 minutes, depending upon age, ability, and class size.

All classes will be limited by the type and number of instruments available. For a private teacher, the size may range from three to eight members. Larger groups could be handled by an individual teacher with previous classroom experience or by a team of two or three teachers, provided that sufficient instruments are available.

No expensive classroom equipment is needed. The piano or spinet organ already in your studio is all that is required. A second instrument permits a larger class; one piano and one spinet organ make a good combination. An electronic keyboard could substitute as a second instrument. The use of rhythm instruments — maracas, tambourine, wrist bells, etc. — is an important aspect of each class.

As class lessons proceed, individual rates of progress become apparent. Often one person develops faster or slower than others in the group. This disparity of progress eventually forces you to reorganize, either by combining different individuals to form a new class, or by disbanding and continuing instead with private lessons.

For additional information, see Chapter 34, "Ages 4-5-6."

CHAPTER 40

IMPROVISING
and CHORD SYMBOLS

This chapter is divided into the following sections:

A. WHAT IS IMPROVISING?

Improvising means spontaneous musical creation — to compose and play at the same time. In its simplest form it means to compose a melody as it is played. It can also mean to simultaneously compose a melody and accompaniment.

More often, improvising means to create a new or varied accompaniment to a known melody as it is played. This type of improvising is usually based on the harmonies suggested by the chord symbols. More sophisticated improvising involves embellishing a known melody with rhythmic variations and by adding extra notes. The accompaniment and melody improvising may be done separately or together and may involve one instrument or several.

B. MYSTERY of IMPROVISING

Unfortunately, improvising can be intimidating. It is often a mystery even to trained musicians because it seems so very different from the comfortable structure of the printed page and conventional training in music theory and harmony. Some musicians outwardly deride improvising, mainly because they can't understand it or can't do it themselves.

Performers who are able to easily improvise harmony and melody are widely admired and sometimes envied. Many people have the mistaken impression that the ability to improvise is largely an inborn talent rather than an acquired skill. Actually, it is a mixture requiring musical talent, analytical work, and lots of practice. Those who are experts at improvising certainly have a keen musical ear, a good musical memory and sense of rhythm, and great technical facility. There is no doubt that the greater these talents, the more potential there is to become good at improvising. What is often overlooked, however, is that improvising can be learned. With proper methods, elements of improvising can be *taught even to students without abundant musical talent.*

C. BENEFITS of IMPROVISING and CHORD STUDY

1. Opportunity for musical creativity
2. Ear training and keyboard harmony
3. Refuge from the strictness of the printed page
4. Personal enjoyment derived from experimentation

Improvising and chord study provide the keyboard teacher with an attractive musical program that can revitalize interest and avoid "musical burn out." Teen-agers and adults will especially enjoy the musical freedom that is offered. Great personal pleasure and satisfaction can be derived from the musical exploration and experimentation involved. Not to be underestimated is the valuable ear training and keyboard harmony experience involved with improvising and chord study.

D. ELEMENTS of IMPROVISING

Most improvising involves a combination of these five basic elements:

1. Rhythmic Variations
2. Added Chord Tones
3. Passing Tones
4. Neighboring Tones
5. Substitute Chords

Individually, each of these elements is easy to understand and learn. They can be taught one at a time starting with very simple applications. The elements can be expanded to very sophisticated sounds and treatments limited only by the musical imagination of the student. The first four elements apply both to accompaniment and melody. The fifth element, substitute chords, applies only to the accompaniment.

E. PRACTICAL TEACHING of IMPROVISING

There have been dozens of books published that attempt to teach improvising. Most of them fail because they try to teach too much, take too much for granted, and progress far too quickly for all but exceptionally talented students. Recent pedagogic developments in a method titled *Easy Keyboard Harmony* by Schaum really make improvising *easier to learn and easier to teach*. However, it is not intended for beginners. The student should have reached at least Level Two before starting improvising work. Basic note reading, rhythms, and musicianship are prerequisites.

The beauty of this pedagogy is its simplicity and great flexibility. *Easy Keyboard Harmony* enables improvising to be taught to students with a wide range of musical aptitudes. Even average students who do not have a musical ear can learn the minimum ideas presented in each book and find them surprisingly satisfying. More talented students are challenged to develop their musical imagination by inventing additional variations. The books are designed to encourage musical creativeness.

For teachers who have never attempted improvising or using chord symbols, the simplicity of this teaching system will be a revelation. For those who have already developed their own improvising skills, *Easy Keyboard Harmony* provides helpful organization, clear explanations, and illustrations needed for effective teaching. Standard chord symbols are used — those commonly found in pop, folk, country, and sacred music — the same as those used for guitar, organ, chord organ, and piano accordion.

Throughout the series of five books, learning is reinforced by writing and playing. The student writes the notes for chords, accompaniments, and improvised patterns on workbook-style pages. Each step is fully explained and illustrated. Students are taught to *spell chords correctly*. Frequent keyboard exercises help develop chord dexterity and ear training.

To gain additional experience and to develop the improvising ideas presented, each book of *Easy Keyboard Harmony* should be supplemented with an album or sheet music containing chord symbols. The *Schaum Piano Teachers Guide* lists numerous choices at various levels. Other chord symbol supplements may be chosen from hundreds of pop, folk, country, and sacred albums or sheet music available in most music stores.

While studying chords and improvising, work should be continued in appropriate method, theory, and technic books. It is intended that improvising will provide an added dimension to a student's music study.

CHAPTER 41

CONTESTS and AUDITIONS

This chapter is divided into these sections:

A. PURPOSE of CONTESTS

Contests, music festivals, and auditions for grade school and high school students are aimed primarily at self-improvement. Although there are elements of competition, the main purpose of the judge is to provide professional evaluation and help rather than criticism. In most contests, students are judged only on *their own* musical proficiency; they are *not* competing with other students. The opportunity for young musicians to hear each other, to learn from their shared experiences, and to stimulate musical achievements is far more important than the grade or rating received.

(For sake of simplicity, the word "contest," as used in the remainder of this chapter, refers also to auditions and music festivals.)

B. WHICH STUDENTS SHOULD PARTICIPATE?

Many contests are limited by age group, musical level, or number of years studied. For example, public school contests often involve only 7th grade through high school. In other contests, the required music often does not include Primer Level, Level One, or Level Two, thereby excluding those students.

Contest success does not necessarily mean getting the highest grade or rating, but it should be a *positive* musical experience. You want your students to benefit from the incentive it provides, but you must be certain it is a *realistic* incentive. You must weigh carefully and candidly each student's chances for reasonable success.

Contests are a special challenge and not necessarily beneficial for all students. They will involve extra work, greater dedication to the keyboard, and a willingness to perform under some stress. You will have to judge which individuals have the best chance of doing well. It is recommended that the student have experience playing in at least two or three recitals before entering a contest. Students who were very nervous or who had difficulty at a recital should not participate until they are more mature, experienced, and confident.

Both you and the student share a risk in the contest results. Those who have a good experience will be motivated to continue their lessons with greater enthusiasm. Contest success is also *valuable publicity for you.* However, those who have difficulty or a traumatic experience at a contest may not only want to quit lessons, but can be damaging to your reputation. Therefore, selecting students for contests is not to be taken lightly.

Students will not always be eager to enter a contest. You will have to take the initiative and in some cases be quite persuasive. Even when you have given considerable care to choosing students, there may be unexpected difficulties or disappointments along the way. If this is the case, in the two or three weeks just before the contest date, you may have to decide to withdraw a student who simply is not meeting your expectations and whose chances for success are marginal. It is far better to withdraw, even at the last minute, than to risk problems at a contest.

C. WHERE TO GET CONTEST INFORMATION

Contests are sponsored by local, county, state, and national music organizations. Some are private groups, others are related to a public institution such as a school system or university. Talent contests are also sometimes sponsored by county parks, religious organizations, and service clubs. Teacher membership is required in the private organizations such as the National Federation of Music Clubs and the National Guild of Piano Teachers. Contests sponsored by a public institution are usually open to students of any private teacher.

Your local music dealer is the first place to ask for contest information. The store may even have a bulletin board for this purpose. Otherwise, your dealer may be able to tell you how to contact musical organizations that are active in your area. Many small towns do not have their own groups, but participate in organizations meeting in larger cities nearby. Music dealers often have in stock the "required" music needed for a contest.

Public and private school music teachers, especially in the intermediate school (junior high) and high school, should also be able to provide information. Of course, your keyboard student must be enrolled and, in some cases, must also be a member of the school band, orchestra, or choir to be eligible to participate.

D. APPLICATION and ENTRY FORMS

Contest dates and entry requirements are usually announced several months in advance. It is advantageous to get all the details as soon as possible. This will give your students adequate time to select and prepare the music.

It is best that YOU take care of submitting the completed entry form, rather than leaving it up to the student or the parents. Find out the **deadline date** for the entry and where it must be sent. Have at least one extra blank entry form on hand in case the first is lost. The entry usually needs your **signature** and may also need the signature of a parent, school principal, band director, or other school official. Your student should be responsible for getting these signatures; be sure to allow plenty of time.

The **entry fee** should be paid by the parents; ask them to give you a check. Be sure that it is properly made out for the correct amount. You can send it along with the entry form.

E. SELECTING MUSIC

There are often several ways a student can participate in a contest or audition. The contest rules may offer one or more of these possibilities:

1. Soloist
2. Accompanist (for a vocal or instrumental solo)
3. Keyboard Ensemble (duet, 2-pianos, etc.)
4. Instrumental Ensemble (with 2 or more wind or string instruments)

If your student is participating only as an accompanist, it is the responsibility of the *soloist* to provide all music, prepare the entry forms, and pay the entry fee. You would be involved only in helping your student learn the accompaniment part. In such case you could skip (in this chapter) to Section G, "How to Prepare Students," and Section I, "Student Advice for Contest Day."

If your student will be a soloist or in a keyboard ensemble read the contest rules carefully! There are often restrictions on the style or composer of music that is permitted. It may be limited to titles on a special list, depending upon the level of the student. Some organizations also restrict the editor and publisher of the music.

Other contests may specify music of certain composers, styles, or musical periods. "Jazz" and "contemporary" are common style requirements. "Baroque," "classic," and "romantic" are examples of musical periods.

It is common for a contest to require original music that is *NOT simplified or arranged.* If you are in doubt, your music dealer may be able to advise you. The *Schaum Piano Teachers Guide* includes special lists of original music as well as jazz, contemporary, American composers, women composers, sonatinas, and other categories which are often mentioned in contest requirements.

F. EXTRA MUSIC for the JUDGE

Find out how many extra copies of the contest music are needed for the judges (sometimes there is a team of judges). If you have the music in your own library, you could loan it for use by the judge. Another possibility is to borrow an extra copy from another student who may have played the same piece last year. If you have two students who are playing the same piece in the contest, they could share the extra copy needed for the judge. Always be sure that it is the *correct edition.* If you are in doubt, consult the contest rules.

If extra copies must be purchased, allow plenty of time *(at least 4 weeks)* in case the music is not in stock at your music dealer. Remember, there are other contestants who will need the same music. When ordering, be very careful to give the full correct title, composer, publisher, and editor (if necessary).

Do NOT make photocopies; *this is a violation of copyright law and may also disqualify the student from participation in the contest or audition.*

Most contests require the measures of music in the judge's copy to be *numbered consecutively.* Music used by the student must also have corresponding numbers. The numbering should be done neatly with pencil. Obviously, the numbers must be the same in all copies.

G. HOW to PREPARE STUDENTS

A student must always have his/her own copy of the contest music in which you can make special notations, comments and reminders as it is being learned. Start work on a contest piece as soon as possible. If you begin early enough, the student can spend three of four weeks learning the basic notes, rhythms, dynamics and phrasing. You can then stop work on the contest piece temporarily for a week or two to give it a rest. Resume work at least three or four weeks before the contest date. During this final work period, you will want to refine the music as much as possible.

Most contests require that a piano soloist play from memory. Therefore, memory work should be started very soon after the notes and rhythm have been learned correctly. It's usually good to memorize a long piece one section at a time, until the whole piece can be played without music. See Chapter 32, "Memorizing."

A cassette tape recorder is highly recommended in contest preparation. It allows the student to hear and evaluate his/her own playing quite objectively. Recordings should be made and studied during the lesson. This allows both of you to make comments and listen again to sections that need attention. Let the student take the cassette home for further listening. The student should be encouraged to make at least one additional recording at home, especially during the final weeks before the contest.

Contest pieces should be polished as much as possible for a good performance. You will want to be more particular than usual with dynamics, phrasing and interpretation. In some cases, you may want to schedule an extra lesson to devote more time to the contest piece. Or you could schedule a 45 or 60 minute lesson instead of a regular 30 minute lesson.

Try to arrange opportunities for your student to perform his/her contest piece at school, in church, or in a recital before the contest. If you have several students involved in the contest, you could arrange a mini-recital in your own studio where they could play for each other and their parents. The experience of playing before an audience, even a small group, is an excellent rehearsal for the contest.

Preparing for a contest should not eclipse other normal keyboard studies. Although there will be emphasis on the contest piece, study should continue in the usual method, technic and theory books. This offers variety to the student during both lesson time and practice.

The student should take a copy of the music along to the contest, even if planning to play from memory. He/she may wish to review in a practice room before playing. Have the student pencil in *every* measure number for the entire piece. Explain that sometimes a judge will ask him/her to repeat a section, beginning at a particular measure number. The judge may also make comments about portions of the music, referring to measure numbers. Obviously, the student must have the music to be able to respond to this.

The student should plan to wear good clothes on the contest day. Both student and parents should be aware of this, and be reminded at least two weeks prior to the contest.

Most contests will inform you of the **time** of the performance for your student. If possible, find out the **name of the building**, which entrance to use and the **room number**. Write this information down on a piece of paper for the student to carry in a purse or wallet to be taken along to the contest.

Be sure to explain the various procedures in Section I, "Student Advice for Contest Day," at the end of this chapter, especially if you are unable to attend the contest yourself.

H. HOW to PREPARE PARENTS

It is helpful, especially if this is the student's first contest, for you to explain to parents the "Purpose of Contests" in Section A, at the beginning of this chapter. Parents sometimes have mistaken notions of what to expect and also need to understand the significance of the grade or rating that will be given by the judge. Occasionally, parents overreact by thinking their child is a genius if a superior rating is received, or by wanting to stop lessons if a mediocre rating is received. As with participation in sports, "you can't win them all" but you always make your best effort.

Encourage an optimistic outlook. Parents who are apprehensive about the contest will probably pass along this anxiety to their child.

Parents should realize that much more practice time than usual will be devoted to the contest piece. Their patience and understanding will help their child do his/her best.

Find out if parents of friends are permitted to hear the students perform. If this is not explained in the contest rules, you may have to ask one of the contest officials. Most contests welcome guests, but sometimes an audience is not allowed. Parents should be encouraged to hear their child perform, if possible. Parental support adds an important psychological boost to the student's performance.

Some students may feel self-conscious or embarrassed if parents or friends are listening. If you think this may be a serious problem at the contest, it is best to talk to the parents beforehand. Perhaps it would be agreeable if they listened outside the contest room.

Most important is that parents **write the date and time for the contest on the family calendar**. Parents should plan to provide transportation to the contest site, arriving at least ONE HOUR before the scheduled time. If the contest is at an unfamiliar location, be sure that they get detailed directions to find it. If it is out of town, they may want to get a street map. It will also help to know what entrance of the building to use. Urge them to allow ample time to find it! If you know of others going to the same contest, you could suggest car pooling. If the contest is sponsored by a public school, there may be a special bus available to transport all students participating in the contest.

Most contests will inform you of the time of your student's performance. If possible, find out the name of the building, which entrance to use and the room number. Convey this information to the parents as soon as possible. Ask that they write it down and carry it with them when going to the contest.

I. STUDENT ADVICE for CONTEST DAY

At the last lesson before the contest it will be very helpful to give the student this advice, especially if you are unable to attend the contest:

1. When you leave home you must have:

- Extra copies of music for the judges.
- Your own copy of the music.
- List showing time and location of your performance.
- Admission ticket or identity form, if required.

2. When arriving at the contest site.

Go to the main information desk. Verify the room number and time, even if they have been given to you in advance. There are sometimes mistakes or last-minute changes in the master schedule. Ask how to find the assigned room — especially if it's in a different building than the information desk.

While at the information desk, find out where the practice rooms and lavatories are located. Ask where the contest results will be posted. If interested, find out if food is available for snacks or lunch and where it's being served. It's also helpful to find the location of a public phone, in case there's someone to call when the contest results are announced!

3. Find the contest room.

Do this immediately after leaving the information desk. Don't enter the room when someone else is playing. Just outside the room there is usually a judge's helper who will be able to tell you if things are on time. You should be mentally prepared to cope with schedule changes. It is possible that things may run behind schedule. If so, the judge's helper will be able to tell your approximate revised performance time. It is a good idea to return to the room once or twice to find out if there are further changes to the schedule.

If there have been cancellations or schedule conflicts, you might be asked to perform early, sometimes on short notice. There is usually no obligation to do this. If you do not feel comfortable performing unexpectedly, you may refuse to play early. However, there are sometimes circumstances where you may be required to play a little sooner than scheduled.

If the room is not being used when you arrive, go in and try out the piano (see section 6 below). Otherwise, go in and sit as an audience for one or two other contestants. (Do NOT enter when someone is playing.) This will enable you to observe the procedure and know what to expect when it is your turn. Most contests have only one judge per room, although sometimes there may be a team of two or three judges.

4. Go to a practice room at least 15 minutes before performing.

Do some warm-up exercises and play through your piece one or two times; then go to the contest room.

5. Be at the contest room at least five minutes before the scheduled time.

Give the judge's helper your name. If there is no helper outside the door (sometimes the helper stays inside), do not enter while someone else is playing. Be sure to have your music, including the necessary judge's copy. If an admittance or identity form is needed, have it ready to give to the helper or to the judge.

6. When it is time for you to play.

The judge's helper will open the door and invite you inside. When you enter, the judge will probably still be writing on the comment sheet of the previous contestant. During this time take the opportunity to:

a. Go to the piano, sit down, and adjust the bench.

b. Push on the pedals to see how hard (or easy) they work.

c. You may play a few measures of your piece (or a warm-up) to sample the touch and feel of the piano. If it is a grand piano, you may have to push harder on the keys. Also try playing something with the soft pedal — on a grand piano it may change the touch of the keyboard.

7. When the judge is ready.

Be sure to give him the "judge's copy" of your music. The helper might announce your name and the title of your piece before you start to play. If not, the judge may ask for your name and the title of your piece. Otherwise, the judge will tell you to begin or simply nod to you as a signal to start.

8. Before you start playing.

Be sure you are comfortable on the bench. Try to really concentrate! It is extremely important that you keep your mind on the music while you are playing. Try to forget about the audience and focus your attention toward doing the best you can!

9. If you make a mistake.

Try very hard to keep on playing and finish the piece. A judge usually forgives a few mistakes, but may not like it if you go back to the beginning and start over, because of the limited time scheduled to each contestant. If you really have difficulty playing from memory, ask the judge if you can use your music.

10. When finished.

Sometimes, the judge may ask you to play a portion of your piece again. If so, you will be told the measure number of where to begin. The judge may sometimes talk to you about your music. Listen carefully and try to remember all of the judge's comments. The judge will also be making written comments on your playing. Wait until your comment sheet has been completed. Before leaving, go over to the judge's table and get your extra music (judge's copy).

The grade or rating of your performance will often be posted on a wall or bulletin board near the audition room, or at a central location. It may take 30 minutes or more for your results to be posted. Sometimes the contest results are not posted, but mailed directly to your teacher. In this case, it may take two weeks or more to get the results.

The written comments and evaluation made by the judge are usually sent directly to your teacher. These may take two weeks or more to arrive.

Abernathy, you're up next!

CHAPTER 42

RECITALS

This chapter is divided into sections that discuss various aspects of recitals:

A. BENEFITS of RECITALS

Presenting your students in a recital is an exciting event. Even though it is extra work for all concerned, there's nothing else that can duplicate your feelings of satisfaction, achievement, and pride as your students perform for an audience!

A recital is important for any teacher because it provides valuable publicity. It displays your teaching capabilities and accomplishments and adds to your professional image. When the program has a good variety of music styles and students of different ages, it shows your versatility as a teacher. Recital publicity is very important and helpful in gaining new enrollments.

For students, a recital experience helps build self-confidence and poise while providing a sense of special pride in the accomplishment. It also teaches the etiquette needed when appearing before an audience.

Students have an opportunity to see and hear each other perform. This experience is valuable and often provides an incentive to learn a piece that someone else has played.

Parents enjoy and take pride in seeing their child perform in front of an audience. It's an opportunity to share this satisfaction by inviting relatives, friends, and neighbors.

A recital gathering affords an ideal time for you to communicate with parents. In a short talk, perhaps at the beginning or midway through the program, you could stress the necessity and importance of parental cooperation in respect to daily practice. Encourage parents with musical skills to play duets and otherwise perform with their own youngsters. This is also an opportunity to remind everyone of the basic benefits of keyboard study. (See Chapter 3, "Benefits of Keyboard Study.")

B. YOUR FIRST RECITAL

You could give a small, informal recital any time after six months of teaching. This could be done with only three or four students. Obviously, the students' playing would take only 10 to 15 minutes. It's recommended that you play one or two solos yourself to round out the program. Since your first program would be quite short, it might be held on a week night rather than a weekend, if the students involved don't have "tons of homework."

Hold the recital in your own home or studio. Invite only the parents, unless you have room for other friends and relatives. Cookies and punch could be served afterward. This is a nice way to expose your students to playing in public, yet keep the audience small and retain a home-like atmosphere.

For information on additional aspects of recital planning, see the list at the beginning of this chapter.

C. WHO SHOULD PARTICIPATE?

Performing for an audience is an important part of musicianship and should be encouraged for all of your students. It's usually easier when started at an early age. Therefore, students who have studied for just three or four months can also participate in a recital. (See Section H, "Ensemble Ideas," later in this chapter.)

Some students will be reluctant to play in a recital and, if given the choice, would probably rather not. Therefore, it's better to make recital participation a *requirement* for all except adults. (However, don't discourage adults from playing. They get just as many benefits from a recital as children do.) You may also make an exception for a teenager, if he would be much older than anyone else on the program. An alternative would be to have a separate "keyboard party" just for teens — or just for adults, even if the group is very small. These students could simply play for one another; an audience is optional.

D. SETTING the DATE and TIME

The date and time for a recital should be set at least two to three months in advance. If you will need to rent a room, it may be necessary to reserve a date five or six months ahead of time. Also plan a rehearsal one or two days before the recital (see Section R, "Rehearsal," later in this chapter).

Check the calendar carefully for possible conflicts with church, school, and community events. Inform parents immediately when you have decided on a date. *Be sure that both recital and rehearsal dates are written on their home calendar.* Tell parents they may bring guests (if you will have adequate seating space). Once the date has been set, stick with it! It's impossible to change the date for one or two families. Put up a big sign in your waiting room or studio six to eight weeks in advance so that all students and parents are constantly aware of the date. It's a good idea to write the date above the title of each student's recital piece so it is in plain view.

Sunday afternoon is usually a good time for recitals. A program beginning at 2:00 is fine, because it allows families time to return home and have lunch after attending church. However, if it is during the football season, check to see that it does not coincide with a game likely to be popular in your area. Otherwise, you will not endear yourself to the fathers in the audience.

Friday or Saturday evenings are other possibilities, but there are more likely to be conflicts because these are popular times for family socializing, and there are also religious services on these evenings. Unless the recital group is very small, a week night is usually not good because it is a school night for the children, many of whom have after-school events and homework.

The time of day will depend partly on the age of your students. If you have a lot of younger children (age 10 and under) an afternoon time is usually best, simply because younger students are not as alert in the evening. If you choose an evening time, start no later than 7:30 and put the youngest ones first on the program.

Two excellent occasions for recitals are at Halloween and Valentine's Day. Because these "holidays" are approximately at mid-semester, there is plenty of time following for new enrollments to be made as a result of the recital publicity. If you teach during the summer months, a program near the end of summer will stimulate September enrollment.

Although very popular, Christmas recitals and end of season programs (in late May or early June) have the disadvantage of competition from many other musical events at the same time. There is also less possibility of gaining additional enrollments at these times.

E. WHERE to HOLD RECITALS

If you have a small number of students and sufficient space in your own home this is the easiest. Otherwise, a church is often a convenient place because its location is known to most people, the seating capacity is adequate, the acoustics are usually good, and the piano is likely to be in good condition. If the church sanctuary is too large or too formal, a church fellowship hall, meeting room, or classroom with a piano might be more suitable for a smaller audience. If you plan to use the church organ in the recital, be sure that the church authorities understand this. In many cases it may also require permission of the church organist. If it is your home church, the church board might allow you to use the room without charge or at a reduced fee, provided that you do the cleaning and straightening up afterwards.

Don't be reluctant to approach a local music store about recital space. You are not obligating yourself by holding a program in a store (unless you accept some special concession). Usually, the rental fee will be considerably less than elsewhere because the dealer profits from the desirable publicity your recital brings. A few retailers even make their recital room available without charge! You're more likely to get a freshly tuned piano at a music store and two or more pianos might be available if you want them.

Retirement homes and nursing homes usually welcome outside groups who are willing to provide entertainment for their residents. Often, there is ample space for families of the students also to be in the audience. Your pupils gain valuable experience and also provide a worthwhile community service. The advantage to you, in most cases, is that the use of the room is free of charge. Of course, be sure that a piano is available and in good working order. As a token of gratitude, you might offer to pay the cost of tuning the piano for the occasion.

Programs can also be held in lodge halls, YMCA's, YWCA's, hotel meeting rooms, or shopping mall community rooms. Other possibilities are motels or restaurants with a large private room, theaters, public school auditoriums or gymnasiums, libraries, and halls belonging to local colleges, unions or veterans groups (American Legion or VFW). Often your city or town hall will have a municipal meeting room available. All of these places usually charge for use of the building including a custodial fee.

If you are renting a room at a restaurant, motel, or lodge, they may require that any refreshments be purchased from them. This may add considerably to the cost, so be sure to ask about it if you plan to serve anything. (See Section Q, "Refreshments," later in this chapter.)

In all cases, *personally try out the instrument before making a decision.* Look and listen especially for tuning and for keys that don't work. On the piano, look for keys that stick, squeaky pedals, and a consistent touch (all keys should sound equally loud when played with equal finger pressure). On the organ, play chromatic scales on all manuals and pedals using one stop at a time. Listen especially for tuning and keys that don't sound in some ranks. If the instrument needs repair the room should be rejected. If the piano needs only tuning you might negotiate for a reduced fee or no fee at all, if you pay for the tuning. Don't rely on promises of the management that the piano will be tuned. Insist on hiring a tuner whom you know to be reliable. If the organ needs tuning, it will depend on how bad it is. A pipe organ is extremely expensive to tune; you should not have to bear that expense. It is usually better to look for a different room. (Also see Section O, "Tuning the Piano and Organ," later in this chapter.)

Many rooms in a restaurant or motel have background music systems. In private rooms this music can usually be turned off, however, it is extremely important that you find out in advance if it can be done. *Insist that you be shown the room with the music turned off.* If the background music cannot be turned off, reject the room.

F. CHOOSING a RECITAL PIECE

A student will perform best when thoroughly prepared. This does not necessarily mean many weeks and months of tedious study on a special recital piece. A recital piece does *not* need to be a student's most difficult achievement. Rather, it should be the piece, or several pieces, which have the best chance of a successful performance.

When a student has developed a repertoire (see chapter 31, "Review Work") you can simply choose several pieces from either the current or previous repertoire. If the student is doing memory work on a regular basis (see Chapter 32, "Memorizing") it is likely that the repertoire choices will already be memorized. It's easy, then, to pick out recital pieces which are comfortable and secure. These have the best chance of success at a recital.

For pupils who seem quite shy and insecure, playing duets is recommended, especially if it's going to be their first recital appearance. Being part of a duet offers the comfort and security of another person coming along and sitting at the keyboard. Most Primer Level Schaum books contain duet accompaniments which are useful in this situation.

Of course, your selections must avoid duplicate music. In a small group, it's embarrassing to the students if the same piece is played more than once.

Knowing your student's personality and special interests will be of great value in helping to choose a recital piece. Some can handle showy music with a fast tempo while others are more comfortable playing something slower. Teen-agers are likely to be more at ease playing pop style music or show tunes. Ideally, a recital piece should be one with which the pupil is comfortably familiar — preferably one of his own favorites. If possible, *let the student choose* from among several pieces. The psychological results can be very rewarding. Chances are, he will work twice as hard if he has chosen his own recital piece.

If you are choosing a new piece for the recital, take great care to pick one that can be done comfortably and is not too ambitious. To save time, you can limit the choice to three or four sheet music pieces at the appropriate level to show and possibly demonstrate, but *let the student make the final choice.* If you have several students who will be getting new recital pieces at about the same time, you may want to pre-select the choices of music and put them in a separate folder for each level.

You will want to start on the recital piece at least two months in advance. Depending upon the progress, you may work for two or three weeks and then give it a rest for a week or two so it doesn't get stale. Give it finishing touches during the last three weeks before the recital.

The *Schaum Piano Teachers Guide* includes many lists of possible recital solos classified by dozens of categories such as, "Animals and Birds," "Circus Music," "Jazz," "Romantic Music," etc. All titles include the level and refer to a page where a thematic sample appears.

G. PROGRAM VARIETY

If your recital will involve six or more students, thought should be given to musical variety. This can be done by selecting from humorous, serious, semi-classical, and pop music. Duets, trios, and other ensembles are excellent. Sing-along participation by the audience also adds variety. All of these elements make the program more appealing to both the performers and the audience.

It is not necessary that the youngest or least proficient students always play at the beginning. An assortment of music, played by students of various ages and levels, makes an attractive variety. Be careful to avoid programming three marches, three waltzes, or three jazz pieces in a row. It is better to scatter them throughout the program. Avoid putting all the boys together or all the advanced pupils in succession. However, be sure to place several advanced students at the end to make a "grand finale."

The *Schaum Piano Teachers Guide* has a large classified section that will provide numerous ideas for different styles of music available for a recital.

H. ENSEMBLE IDEAS

Ensembles add variety and sparkle to any recital. When one piano is used, try duets (1 piano, 4 hands) and trios (1 piano, 6 hands). The *Schaum Piano Teachers Guide* lists many suggestions. If you are fortunate enough to have two pianos available, there are many additional opportunities.

An excellent way to add audience appeal is to present different family members together (in ensemble) at a recital. This is great publicity for you since it gives a very desirable image of "family togetherness" achieved via keyboard study. It's fun to have a duet with two children playing together or parent and child together. Often one of your keyboard students may also be studying another instrument. You could have that student play a piano solo and also a clarinet solo with you as the accompanist. If another family member plays a different instrument this could be combined into a duet or ensemble. For example, your pupil plays a piano accompaniment to his father's trumpet solo.

It's amazing how other adults in the audience will react when they see another parent performing with his child. You may even stimulate other parents to start keyboard lessons themselves!

For younger students, an ensemble of rhythm band instruments (drum, wood block, triangle, castanets, etc.) along with piano or organ is good fun!

Organ and piano may often be combined into ensembles when you have both instruments available. You will find arrangements where an organ solo can be combined with a piano solo to make an organ-and-piano duet. Often, piano solos have printed chord symbols. The pianist can play the solo as written while the organ student improvises an accompaniment from the chord symbols, or vice-versa.

An excellent project for a group of piano teachers is to stage a multi-keyboard recital. This may consist of any number of pianos and/or organs from four to 100. It is produced with the cooperation of a keyboard dealer who furnishes the instruments as a publicity effort.

I. SHOWMANSHIP and NOVELTIES

Costume recitals are great fun for all and costumes help students to be more relaxed (they're often more concerned about the costume than about their playing)! The best occasion is just before Halloween because many students normally have trick-or-treat costumes. It's not necessary that every student play Halloween music, although it is desirable when possible. The motif (or "theme") is the important thing. There could be special invitations or programs on orange paper (perhaps cut in the shape of a pumpkin) and decorations in the room or on the keyboard suggesting Halloween.

Other motifs or "themes" for a recital are sports, a circus, Valentine's Day, an imaginary trip around the world, animals, etc. All offer opportunities for costumes and decorations. Where possible, the choice of music should also fit the motif.

Nearly always, the birthday of a pupil or one of his relatives will fall near the recital date. This gives an opportunity to use the Schaum sheet music solo, *Birthday Bouquet,* a set of variations on the familiar birthday theme. This is available as a piano solo, piano duet, and an organ solo.

A recital is much more effective if there is some occasional humor. This can be accomplished by having some students "dress the part" of the music they are playing. This involves the use of a full or partial costume, "props," or posters. The prop can be placed on the piano or nearby table while playing. For example, a boy playing a cowboy piece could wear a cowboy hat. A student playing an astronaut or "Star Wars" piece could carry a model space ship or wear a toy space helmet. Someone playing *Little Dog Boogie* could carry a stuffed dog. With a little imagination, most students can invent many similar ideas. All of this makes the time more fun for the audience and helps the performers be more relaxed.

Sing-alongs involving the audience are effective, especially with familiar songs. Different students can play the accompaniment for different songs. This provides valuable accompaniment experience to the student. (It is usually best to play *with music.*)

A project involving a keyboard dealer and group of teachers is a "keyboard marathon" lasting between two and four hours. The best location is an indoor shopping mall; the best time is on a Saturday or Sunday afternoon. Both piano and organ could be involved. This provides marvelous publicity both for the dealer and teachers involved. Each teacher should have one or two large posters made saying, "keyboard students of (Your Name)." Your address and telephone number could also be included. These posters would be put on easels and placed conspicuously so they could be seen by the audience from at least two sides during the time your students are performing.

A marathon project requires a lot of careful organizing and scheduling. Obviously, it requires the consent and help of the shopping mall management. The dealer is usually glad to help with newspaper publicity and furnishing instruments. This event provides a unique experience for your students and gives important public exposure to keyboard music.

Let one student or an adult act as "master-of-ceremonies" at the recital. If you have a small number of pupils (ten or less), this person could introduce each performer, telling a little about where the student is from, how long he has been studying, and something about the music being played. A few musical anecdotes and other tasteful jokes, especially something relating to the title of the music being played, might be used for variety. Otherwise, the main purpose of the emcee is to warm up the audience and help relax the students at the beginning. Care must be taken not to overshadow the performers. This requires someone who can think fast, is tactful, and has a pleasant personality. Don't try it unless you have an individual who can do it well.

J. HOW to PREPARE STUDENTS

All students should try to play their recital piece from memory. Therefore, memory work should be started very soon after the notes and rhythm have been learned correctly. It's usually good to memorize a long piece one section at a time, such as two lines per week or four lines per week, until the whole piece can be played from memory.

Students should be told that if they play some wrong notes, they should try to keep calm and continue playing. Your own reactions are vitally important here. If you maintain a calm attitude, the student is likely to do the same. Explain that most people in the audience will not notice a few wrong notes, but it will be very obvious if the pupil tries to correct the wrong notes or tries to start over. This is a good habit of musicianship that should be encouraged when playing at lessons and at all times when performing.

If there is a lapse of memory in the middle of a piece, the student should try to continue playing by skipping (either ahead or behind) to a familiar section in the music. Again, maintaining a level headed attitude is essential. The student should not be made to feel hopeless or desperate because of memory failure.

A cassette tape recorder is highly recommended in recital preparation. The recital piece should be recorded at least three weeks before the recital. It's remarkable how errors in rhythm, dynamics, phrasing, pedaling, etc. suddenly become clear to the student when listening to his/her own recording. Let the student take the cassette home for further listening. The student should be encouraged to make at least one additional recording at home, especially during the final weeks before the recital.

Recital pieces should be polished as much as possible for a good performance. You will want to be more particular than usual with dynamics, phrasing and interpretation. If necessary, you could schedule an extra lesson. Or you could schedule a 45 or 60 minute lesson instead of the usual 30 minute lesson.

Preparing for a recital should not eclipse other regular keyboard studies. Although there will be emphasis on the recital piece, study should continue in the usual method, technic and theory books, but with shorter assignments during recital preparation. This offers variety to the student both during lesson time and during practice.

Students and their parents should be told well in advance (five to six weeks) to plan to wear good clothes. It is not necessary to buy a special outfit for the occasion, but the clothes should look nice. You may want to send a note home to parents regarding appropriate recital attire.

About two weeks before the recital, it's a good idea to show the student how to approach the piano, leave the piano and acknowledge applause. If a photographer will be taking individual pictures after each performance, the student should be told to wait alongside the instrument (holding the prop, if any) until the photo is taken. The student may even want to practice this at home.

K. PUBLICITY

If the number of participants is small and the audience space is limited, "word of mouth" contact with each parent is sufficient publicity. However, *remind* the students at their lessons and *write* the recital date and time in the assignment book at least twice. A reminder phone call to parents, about three weeks before the recital date, is helpful. If there is sufficient space, also remind parents that they are welcome to bring as many guests as they like.

When you have room for a larger audience, you could have printed recital invitations made. These could be on colored 3x5 cards in the form of a "ticket." Be sure all essential information is listed: date, place, time, and other necessary details. (For example, if refreshments will be served afterward.) Give eight to ten invitations to each student to pass out among friends and relatives. These should be circulated at least two to three weeks prior to recital time. The printing should be the neatest you can afford. Although mimeograph work is inexpensive, you should also check prices and see samples of print quality at a "quick print" shop. If your program will be at a church, they might let you use the printing equipment in the church office. Incidentally, this is an excellent form of advertising for yourself!

For seasonal recitals such as Halloween, Christmas, Valentine's Day, etc., the invitation could be on colored paper or printed with colored ink or cut into the shape of a pumpkin, bell, heart, piano, etc.

Posters could be made announcing the recital. Homemade posters are perfectly all right. Perhaps you have a student with a flair for art work who might design posters for you. If you are affiliated with a school or church, perhaps these organizations would allow you to put up a poster on their premises. Sometimes a music store will let you put up a poster in their window.

Local, community, and neighborhood newspapers, especially those with weekly or bi-weekly distribution, are often glad to publish articles when they include the names of participating students. You can also send along a photo of yourself or of one of your students. If a student is in costume, or parent and child will perform together, such photos are particularly desirable. Usually this is considered a news or society item, for which there is no charge. Your article is more likely to be published if you can provide a neatly type-written (double-spaced) list of student names along with where and when the recital will be held.

Another possibility is to mail out invitations to every house in your neighborhood within a radius of one or two miles. A city or community directory or chamber of commerce might have lists of house numbers with the names of their occupants. To save the cost of addressing and postage, the invitations can be distributed as handbills. It is best to simply roll up a sheet of paper and attach it to a door knob with a rubber band. Technically, you are not permitted to deposit anything in a home-owner's mail box unless postage has been paid.

L. LENGTH of RECITALS

Programs of moderate length are best; 45 minutes to one hour is ideal. Write down the time and title of each student's pieces during a lesson. Any clock with a second hand may be used. Add approximately one-half minute between each performer for applause and going to and from the keyboard. This will give you a pretty close estimate of the program length.

There are several factors to consider when deciding on how long the recital should be:

1. Younger children, age 10 and below, have difficulty sitting still and will become restless and sometimes distracting if compelled to stay in the same seat too long. The more youngsters on the program, the shorter it should be.

2. Those pupils who are performing toward the end of the program have a longer wait — thus a longer time to nurture their nervousness. The maturity of the students near the end of the program should also be considered.

3. Parents and relatives are primarily interested in hearing their own child. Sometimes the family may have another activity scheduled for later on the same day. Keeping adults in the audience happy is another important factor.

4. The amount of musical variety and showmanship on the program is a measure of its audience appeal. Programs with more variety can be somewhat longer.

If there will be 20 or more pupils on a program it is likely to run more than 45 minutes. If you have a large group of students, divide them into two separate programs on the same day. For example, schedule one at 2:00 PM and another at 3:30 or 4:00 PM on the same afternoon. Another possibility is to have refreshments served during an intermission about halfway through the program. Those who feel they are not able to stay for the entire program could leave during the intermission. This enables you to keep programs of reasonable length and still present a large number of students.

M. AWARDS and GIFTS

A recital is a unique opportunity to give recognition to students for good work and special accomplishments. The recognition is all the more valuable because it is done *in front of an audience.* The positive effects of any award are magnified when presented at a recital. This can be a tremendous ego boost to a student!

Simply performing in a recital is worthy of recognition. Each student can be given an award certificate that is inexpensive and effective. Schaum Publications offers two all-purpose certificates printed on parchment-style paper (these are illustrated on pages 105 and 106); both are sizes for which common picture frames are available .

5 x 7 inches: *Certificate of Musical Merit*

8 x 10 inches: *Certificate of Musical Achievement*

A brief ceremony, at the end of the recital, could have each pupil come forward to accept this award, as you read his name.

In addition to recital participation, certificates can be awarded for:

1. Completion of all materials at one level.

2. Participation in a contest, music festival, or audition.

3. Completion of a special unit such as a sonatina, sonata movement, accompaniment work for a soloist or group.

4. Participation in their fifth or tenth recital.

5. Perfect lesson attendance for the semester or season.

Certificates for these and other special achievements can be dressed up by affixing the *Schaum Gold Award Seal.* Major accomplishments can be recognized by adding a narrow piece (¼ to ⅜ inch wide) of colored ribbon about four to five inches long. Fold the ribbon into an upside-down V-shape and attach to the certificate by placing the gold seal on top of the point of the "V."

Many teachers like to present their pupils with a small gift during a recital. The following items published by Schaum are suitable and economical (see Chapter 51, "Teaching Aids, Dictionaries, and Flash Cards") :

Lesson Assignment Book

Chord Dictionary

Music Dictionary

Practice Poster

Other inexpensive gift ideas are a piece of sheet music and special imprinted pencils that say, "Student of (Your Name)."

For major achievements, you may want to consider a corsage or boutonniere to be worn at the recital. Music boutique items such as plaques, pins, statuettes, medals, etc. are other possibilities. However, because of the cost you will want to be sure the achievement is worthy of the gift.

Arrange for a photographer to take a group photo and/or individual photos at the recital. It is effective to take individual pictures immediately after each performance. As the pupil is acknowledging the applause, he should pause briefly (holding the prop, if any) to allow the photographer to snap the photo. This procedure should be practiced during the rehearsal. Those who want prints as a souvenir may purchase them from the photographer. Often, a professional photographer will come at no charge to you, since he profits from the prints that are sold. Another possibility is to arrange for the entire recital to be videotaped, then make copies of the tape available for purchase. These ideas are especially effective at costume recitals.

N. ROOM LAYOUT and SEATING

Careful room layout will help make your recitals more effective. Obviously, the keyboard should be the center of attention in the room and should be in "concert position" so that the performer looks at the audience over his *right* shoulder. Be sure to eliminate any distracting backdrops, posters, pictures, etc. around the keyboard. The chairs for the audience should be positioned so they face *away from* the entrance to the room. Otherwise, late-comers will seriously distract from the program.

Many teachers like to have their students sit together at the front of the room, near the keyboard. If they are seated in their order of performance this will minimize commotion as one student finishes and the next begins. The object is to keep things moving with as little delay as possible between each piece. You may have signs or colored ribbons at the ends of each row, reserving the necessary seats for students only.

If you have rented a room, be sure that seats are included. Unless it is a theater or auditorium where the seats are fastened to the floor, you will have to tell the manager or custodian how many seats you will need and how they should be arranged. If there is plenty of space, leave at least six inches of space between each seat and ample leg room between each row of seats.

Be sure to allow ample aisle space; ideally the aisle should get wider toward the back of the room. Two aisles are usually better than one, if you have the space. Safe and fast exit in an emergency should be kept in mind. Do not place chairs where they block an aisle or exit door. Keep exit doors clear and be sure they can be opened from the inside. This is particularly important when you are likely to have a large crowd. If you have rented a room or hall and find an exit door locked or blocked, insist that it be cleared and unlocked before your program begins. Find out the location of the nearest telephone in case of emergency.

Keeping the keyboard close to the audience is an advantage. A close-knit feeling gives greater intimacy, more casualness, and makes the situation less intimidating to the student. Encourage the audience to sit near the front of the room. Where possible, avoid putting the pupils on a stage or high platform unless the expected audience will be quite large.

If any of the students will be using props (see Section I, "Showmanship and Novelties," earlier in this chapter) there should be a small table near the piano on which to place the prop while playing. A card table is fine. To be more dressy, add a skirt to the table in a color suited to the season or occasion.

You may want to purchase a "Guest Book" or use sheets of paper for a guest list. It makes the guests feel special and, after the recital, you will enjoy relaxing and seeing who was there. If you expect a large crowd it is better to have two or three separate registration lists so that several people can sign the list at once. You will want one or two volunteers to assist the guest registration by showing people to the registration table and passing out programs. A table and pens should be placed near the entrance to the room. You may get some leads for future students from the guest list.

O. TUNING the PIANO and ORGAN

As mentioned previously in Section E, "Where to Hold Recitals," it's extremely important that you try out the instruments in the room before signing a rental agreement. If the piano or organ needs repair, reject the room and look elsewhere. If the piano needs only tuning, you could negotiate for a reduced room rental fee (or no fee at all) in exchange for your paying the tuner. If you plan to use the organ, also check the tuning. Most electronic organs do not require tuning, but there are a few brands, especially older models, that do need tuning. If it is a pipe organ, you'll need to check the tuning of all ranks which your students will use. If the organ needs tuning badly, it is usually best to look for a different room. Pipe organ tuning is very expensive; you should not offer to pay or even share the cost of tuning a pipe organ unless it is your home church and you can afford to treat it as a contribution.

Scheduling the piano tuner should be done as soon as the date of your recital has been confirmed. Ideally, the piano should be tuned just one or two days before the recital. It is also very important that the piano *not be moved after it has been tuned*. Some instruments are quite sensitive and moving just a few feet will cause them to go out of tune. If you will be using piano and organ together, be sure the tuner is instructed to *tune the piano with the organ*. If the organ is not in tune, it is better to tune the piano to normal pitch and not play the instruments together.

If you're renting a room, don't rely on promises of the management to get a tuner. Insist on hiring your own tuner who you know to be reliable and who can get the job done in time for your recital. Set an appointment for the tuning with the manager or person in charge of renting the room. Find out if there are other activities scheduled in the room between the time the piano is tuned and your recital. If so, insist that the piano *not be moved before your recital.*

P. PRINTED PROGRAMS

Printed programs are useful in several ways:

1. To organize and add prestige to the recital
2. As a source of pride for both parent and child, who enjoy seeing their name in print
3. As a memento or souvenir
4. As advertising for you, the teacher! Encourage families to take extra copies to send to relatives and show to neighbors

Start writing down the titles of music and students' names at least *three weeks before* the recital. If you have a home computer, decide on the program format and enter in the titles and names to form a tentative program. The sequence can easily be rearranged as needed. Otherwise, use 3x5 index cards for the same purpose.

At least *two weeks in advance*, decide on where the programs are to be printed. Local copy/print shops that make photocopies are usually the most economical. It does pay to shop around for the best price, but ask to see printed samples that you can judge for neatness. Some shops will make copies while you wait or allow you to run the copy machine yourself. Otherwise, find out how long it will take to have them completed. Be sure you understand the full cost of the copies you need. Often there is a minimum quantity required for the best price.

The final copy of your program should be made on a good quality computer printer or typewriter. Be sure to have the time and date, including the year. Have someone else check it over with you for omissions, spelling errors (especially student names) and possible duplicate titles.

If you have no computer or typewriter, a friend or parent of one of your students may be able to transcribe a handwritten copy for you. Otherwise this could usually be done at the copy/print shop for an additional charge. In any case, be sure to carefully proofread the transcribed copy by comparing it to your handwritten copy.

When there is extra space on the program, you could add an announcement or advertisement. A note on audience etiquette could be included, politely telling people to be courteous, listen attentively and wait with flash cameras until after the program. You might want to announce the date of your next recital. If you are offering lessons to adults or adding additional time to your teaching schedule, this could also be mentioned on the program.

Plan that there be enough programs so that each performer will have his/her own copy plus *at least* two copies per family in the audience. You may need additional copies if grandparents and neighbors are expected.

To add a professional touch, print your programs on one of the *Schaum Recital Program Blanks*. There are many colorful cover designs including several for Christmas. The blanks are 8½ x 11 inches and designed to be folded in half to 5½ x 8½. After folding, the design becomes the front cover. The remainder of the sheet is blank for printing your students names, titles, dates, location, etc. The *Recital Program Blanks* are available in packages of 25 or 50 sheets. The paper will work in any copy machine or computer printer that accepts plain paper.

Homemade program designs are also effective. If you are not artistically inclined, perhaps a friend or student with artistic talent could create musical or seasonal decorations for the program. Programs can be printed on different colors of paper. There are also many specialty papers with fun designs and patterns available at art supply or stationery stores.

Be sure to enlist someone as a volunteer to help pass out programs as the audience enters the room.

Q. REFRESHMENTS

Simple refreshments such as cookies or cake and punch are a nice way to end a program and also serve as a tangible reward, especially for the younger children. Often, several mothers may be willing to help furnish the baked goods. Inexpensive punch could either be poured out of a can over ice or made with a recipe. Be sure to provide small plates and napkins.

If you are renting a room at a restaurant, motel, or lodge, they may require that any refreshments be purchased from them. This may add considerably to the cost, so be sure to inquire. They may be willing to furnish the serving table and tablecloth without extra charge. If not, the table can be covered depending upon your budget.

Table decorations can be simple and inexpensive. A dried flower arrangement or musical nicknacks from your home are possibilities. Depending on the time of year, seasonal decorations may be appropriate. If the recital has a motif or "theme" the decorations could fit in with that theme. Lighted candles, if they are positioned safely away from flammables and supervised by an adult, add a touch of elegance.

R. REHEARSAL

When you set a date for a recital, also plan a rehearsal one or two days before the performance. This is particularly important if the location is away from your studio and the instrument will not be the same as that used for lessons. A short, informal rehearsal gives each student an acquaintance with the recital instrument and environment. It also contributes to their self-assurance and success.

Try to hold the rehearsal at the *same time of day* as the recital is scheduled. The lighting plays a big part in the success of the program. Unwanted sunlight, especially that which interferes with the vision of the performers, should be controlled with drapes, shades or blinds. If the program is at night, extra lamps may be needed at the keyboard for those using music. In a rented room you may need help from a custodian to locate the switches for the lights you need. If the room is in a restaurant or hotel with a background music system, be sure that the music is turned off during your recital.

Students should bring all props and costumes (if any) and use them at the rehearsal. This is the time to find out if there is a mask or part of the costume (particularly long, flowing sleeves) that may interfere with playing at the keyboard.

During the rehearsal, students should be coached on recital routine, etiquette, and behavior:

1. Remind students that they are to wear good clothes for the occasion.

2. Students should be shown where to sit in the first two or three rows of seats so they will be *in sequence as they will play on the program.* This minimizes delay between each individual performance.

3. If students are to enter the room as a group, they should be lined up in their seating sequence and shown how to walk in an orderly and quiet manner.

4. Courtesy must be emphasized. Tell students to sit attentively and quietly until it is their turn to perform. Even while they are waiting, they should not slouch in their seats. They should respect the efforts of other students by not talking or causing a distraction during any playing. Students must be warned *not to laugh* if someone else makes a mistake. After all, it could happen to anyone. If they want to talk between performances, it should be done very quietly.

5. Instruct the students that there is to be NO GUM CHEWING! There is nothing more distracting than watching a pupil try to chew gum in rhythm to his playing.

6. When it is his turn to play, each student should make an orderly approach to the keyboard — not too hastily. Instruct him to approach the bench from the *left* and leave from the right. Urge him to take time to adjust the bench and find a comfortable seating position before starting. It would be very helpful for you to demonstrate both the correct and incorrect ways. If possible, props should be kept under each student's seat until used. If the prop is too large, you or another pupil will have to keep it handy and give it to the performer as he approaches the keyboard. He should practice taking the prop up front and placing it on a table next to the piano.

7. Boys and girls should be shown how to acknowledge applause gracefully with a bow, curtsy or nod. When finished playing, students should stand, move away from the keyboard, face the audience and pause briefly to acknowledge applause. If a photographer will be taking individual pictures, they should stand and wait (with prop in hand, if any) alongside the instrument for the photographer to take the picture. Students should not run back to their seats too quickly. Again, it is helpful if you demonstrate how to do this for both boys and girls. Most children should simply return to their assigned seats at the front of the room and remain there until the recital is finished. However, it is better that young children, ages 4-5-6, and others who are likely to get wiggly or noisy, sit with their parents when they have finished playing.

8. When a student is playing several short pieces, the audience should be asked to hold its applause until all pieces are finished. You will have to make this announcement at the beginning of the program. This makes it easier for the student to acknowledge the applause and helps the program move along faster and more smoothly.

9. It's very important to tell your students, "It's OK to be nervous." Many pupils may be uptight at the rehearsal, especially if this is their first recital. One of the main reasons students are nervous is because they are afraid of the unknown and don't know what to expect. The rehearsal is a considerable help in relieving such fears. Mention some of the typical symptoms – cold hands, sweaty hands, a dry mouth, queasy stomach – and emphasize that such symptoms are perfectly normal and happen to almost all performers – including you! It will be very reassuring to the student to know that nearly everyone shares these discomforts and that this is a sign that the student is especially alert, can think more quickly and probably do his/her best work.

10. Students should be told what to do if they make mistakes or if their memory slips during the middle of a piece. They should try to keep calm and continue playing, if possible. It is far better to keep playing, even with some wrong notes, than to stop completely and try to start over. Often the audience may not notice just a few wrong notes. But it will be very obvious if the student stops in the middle and restarts. (See Section J, "How to Prepare Students," in this chapter.)

At the rehearsal you may have to make a decision regarding playing from memory. If the student falters during the rehearsal, you might ask that he plan to use his music at the recital. During the performance, they might not actually look at the music at all. However, just the security of having the music available often makes the difference between a success and an embarrassing memory lapse. Although playing from memory is preferred, it's perfectly all right for those who have difficulty memorizing to use their music at a recital. It's far better to do a good job with music than to risk a memory failure.

S. CHECK LIST for PREPARATIONS

There are many things to do in the weeks preceeding a recital. It is best to prepare a list of things to be done in sequence and check them off as they are completed. Although you may be a very organized person, a check list is very comforting, especially if you have not presented many recitals. This may eliminate some last minute rushing to complete something that was overlooked. When you have things well organized, it will make the recital day much more enjoyable for you.

(continued on next page)

Ten to Twelve Weeks Before Recital Date:

1. Set the Date and Time of Recital and Rehearsal.
2. Reserve Room or Hall, if necessary.
3. Schedule Piano Tuner, if necessary.
4. Schedule Photographer (optional).
5. Schedule Video-Tape Operator (optional).
6. Tell Parents to Put Recital and Rehearsal Dates on Family Calendar.
7. Choose Motif or "Theme" (optional).
8. Select Recital Pieces for Each Student.

Six Weeks Before Recital Date:

9. Plan Decorations (home-made or purchased).
10. Order Recital Invitation Cards.
11. Plan and Purchase Award Certificates.
12. Plan Gifts (optional, home-made or purchased).

Four Weeks Before Recital Date:

13. Distribute Invitation Cards.

Three Weeks Before Recital Date:

14. Prepare Write-up and Photo for Newspaper Publicity.

Two Weeks Before Recital Date:

15. Plan and Order Printed Programs.
16. Plan Rehearsal, Remind Students about it.
17. Purchase Guest Book or Plan Sign-up Sheets (optional).
18. If program is to be recorded, check to see that the cassette machine works. Buy blank cassette tapes. Buy new batteries, if necessary.

One Week Before Recital Date:

19. Wrap Gifts, if any.
20. Fill In Name, Date, etc. on Award Certificates.

Three Days Before Recital:

    21. Pick Up Printed Programs.

    22. Pack Tote Bag with "Emergency" Supplies: Safety Pins, Scotch® Tape, Kleenex®, Band Aids®, Scissors, Aspirin, etc.

Rehearsal Day:

    23. Plan to arrive at the rehearsal at least 30 minutes before the scheduled time. See that the room is set up properly.

Recital Day:

    24. Instruct students to arrive at least 30 minutes before the scheduled time. If a group picture is planned, have students arrive 45 or 50 minutes early so the group picture can be taken before the recital begins.

(Space for Personal Memos)

CHAPTER 43

TAX HINTS
(Revised June 1998)

Many music teachers pay unnecessary taxes simply because they are not aware of the deductions that may be legally claimed. This article lists some ways in which you may be able to save money on taxes.

Because of different tax laws in each state and constant revisions and rulings on tax laws, the suggestions here may not apply to you. Your own marital status, other income, number of dependents and new tax laws may also influence the application of these ideas to your situation. If there is any doubt, consult with a knowledgeable tax advisor when preparing your tax returns. In some cases you may also need the advice of a tax attorney.

It is very important to *keep receipts for all expenses*. If the receipt does not describe the items purchased you should write, on the back of the receipt, a brief description of what you bought. Be sure the receipt has the complete date and the name and address of the store or business. Cancelled checks, if used, should also be kept, but it is best to have a receipt in addition to the check. If items are paid for by credit card, such as MasterCard or Visa, be sure to save all the credit card vouchers and all monthly statements issued by the credit card company. You need to have an invoice or receipt to identify what the check or credit card voucher paid for. All receipts, cancelled checks, credit card vouchers, etc. should be saved for at least four years and until you are certain that your tax return will not be audited. Receipts for real estate and equipment should be kept for four years after the date of disposal or sale.

Expenditures for the following items are usually deductible for tax purposes when adequate records and receipts are kept:

ADVERTISING such as:

Business Cards	Program Aids	Newspaper Ads
Promotional Letters	Outdoor Signs	Solicitation

CHILD CARE SERVICES. If you have young children that need a baby sitter during the time you teach, you will need to comply with Social Security withholding requirements for employees in the home.

BOOKS and RECORDINGS. Items that relate to your continued musical education or that are used as reference materials in your teaching, such as:

Cassette Recordings	Compact Discs
Reference Books	Record Albums

Music Biographies / Dictionaries / Textbooks

CLEANING SERVICES. If you hire someone to help clean your house, the portion of time spent cleaning your studio and waiting room. You will need to comply with Social Security withholding requirements for employees in the home.

COMPUTER SOFTWARE. The cost of software that is used *exclusively* for music. This would include software used for music education, remedial work, tutorials and music appreciation. Also software used *exclusively* for keeping your teaching records and finances.

CONCERT TICKETS. The cost of tickets for professional recitals, concerts and musical performances that relate to your continued musical education.

HOUSEHOLD SUPPLIES. Items that are used by students in your waiting room and bathroom, such as:

Kleenex®	Paper Towels	Toilet Tissue
Light Bulbs	Soap	

INSURANCE. The extra cost of insuring your instrument, accessories and equipment needed in teaching. The extra cost of insuring your personal car for business use. Premiums for liability insurance needed for operating a business in your home.

MAINTENANCE and REPAIRS for instruments, amplifier/speaker, cassette recorder and stereo system, such as overhauling, cleaning and piano tuning.

MUSIC MAGAZINE SUBSCRIPTIONS. Magazines that relate to your continued musical education and help maintain your skills as a musician.

MUSIC ORGANIZATION MEMBERSHIPS. Dues for professional musical groups, guilds at local, state or national levels.

MUSICAL SUPPLIES such as:

Assignment Books	Cork Grease	Mouthpieces
Award Certificates	Flash Cards	Reeds
Award Seals	Keyboard Chart	Rosin
Blank Cassette Tapes	Ligature	Slide Oil
Cleaning Swabs	Manuscript Paper	Valve Oil

POSTAGE. Stamps used for the mailing of advertising, billings, greeting cards and recital announcements.

REAL ESTATE TAX. If a room in your home is used *exclusively* for teaching, you may be able to deduct a proportionate amount of the property tax on your house. This is usually based on the area of the teaching room and its proportion to the total livable area of your home.

When a room in your home is used *exclusively* for teaching, you may also be able to depreciate a percentage of the purchase price of your home, based on the area of the teaching room with relation to the total area of the home. Your tax advisor will be able to provide further information.

RECITAL EXPENSES such as:

Award Certificates	Gifts	Prizes
Chair Rental	Invitations	Programs
Custodial Fees	Photographs	Recording
Decorations	Piano Moving	Room Rental
Flowers	Piano Tuning	Tickets

RECORD KEEPING. The Schaum *Weekly Lesson Report* sheet is a good way to keep track of income received from each student. Be sure to make entries on these report sheets every week, especially as lessons are paid. These lesson report sheets will be valuable in determining your total income for the year.

Your deductible expenses should be recorded in detail and you should retain receipts and cancelled checks as proof of expenditures. A diary or weekly schedule book, with entries maintained as they occur, giving the date, purpose, location and persons and places involved is very convincing proof on the occasion of tax audits.

REMODELING. If you have one room in your home that is used *exclusively* for teaching, the expenses of remodeling, including paint, wallpaper, carpeting, drapes, light fixtures, shelves, etc. may be deducted.

If remodeling is significant in magnitude and cost, the expense may have to be capitalized and recovered through depreciation. If, on the other hand, you rent space outside of your home for teaching, the rent and any other costs related to the rented space, are deductible as a current expense.

RETIREMENT. Whether you are married or single, thought should be given to savings for your eventual retirement. There are presently several popular forms of IRA (Individual Retirement Account) plans that encourage savings for retirement. A portion of your self-employed earnings as a music teacher may be set aside in an IRA each year. Depending on the IRA plan you choose, your marital status and your income, there are differing options for tax deductions. There are also numerous investment opportunities for IRA funds. Consult your tax advisor for information on the best plan for your situation.

STATIONERY and OFFICE SUPPLIES such as:
Birthday cards, get-well cards and holiday cards sent to your students.

Billing Forms	Labels	Schedule Books
Envelopes	Letterheads	Typewriter Supplies
File Folders	Receipt Books	

STUDIO EQUIPMENT, such as:

Bulletin Board	Rubber Stamps
Calculator	Scissors
Chalk Board	Scotch® Tape Dispenser
Clock	Shelves
Ink Pad	Stapler
Paper Punch	Ruler
Pencil Sharpener	

STUDIO SUPPLIES, such as:

Calendar	Paper Clips
Chalk	Pencils
Colored Ball Points	Rubber Bands
Eraser	Scotch® Tape
Kleenex®	Staples
Marking Pens	

TRAVEL TO and FROM STUDENT'S HOMES.

If a separate studio is rented away from the home then travel to and from the home to the studio is not deductible. Travel from the studio for any business purpose and back to the studio is deductible.

If a room in the home is used exclusively as a teaching studio and most of the students come there for lessons, then travel to and from a student's home to give lessons (for example, a handicapped child) would be deductible because the studio at the home would be a place of business.

IRS rulings on mileage allowances do change from one year to the next. Consult your tax advisor for the latest information.

UTILITIES. The portion of the costs of heat and electricity for a room that is used *exclusively* for teaching may be deducted. A portion of telephone and water costs may also be deducted if a satisfactory formula is made for determining those portions.

DEPRECIATION. Your teaching is considered a small business for tax purposes and you are subject to various rules and regulations affecting small business. You need to choose *expensing* or *depreciating* of business equipment. This choice depends upon which method of tax deduction offers the most savings in the current year *and* in future years. There is also the possibility that a large purchase may be partly *expensed* and partly *depreciated*. There are limitations and conditions. You should consult a qualified tax advisor when deciding upon which method is best for you.

Usually, your teaching equipment costs under $50.00 per item should be treated as a business expense with the entire amount used as a tax deduction in the same year as the purchase. This method of deduction is called *expensing*.

Equipment purchases larger than $50.00 per item are usually depreciated, if it creates a tax savings. *Depreciating* means that tax deductions for the purchase cost of equipment are spread out over several years. An *allowable life* must be determined for each piece of equipment that is depreciated. The *allowable life* is the number of years that the equipment can reasonably be expected to function before wearing out or becoming obsolete. The government publishes listings of the allowable life for various items.

For example, if the allowable life is five years, tax deductions of the purchase cost of the equipment must be spread out over five years. The amount deducted in each of the five years varies according to a *schedule* of percentages established by the IRS. If the allowable life is seven years, your tax deductions would be spread out over seven years, using a 7-year IRS schedule. These depreciation schedules are published in the tax return forms for small businesses.

Generally, the allowable life for electronic equipment such as a computer is five years. Other equipment, such as a piano or furniture would have an allowable life of seven years.

It is extremely important to keep receipts of your equipment purchases and also to prepare a depreciation schedule showing the allowable life and how much you are deducting each year for each piece of equipment. In the event of an audit, you would have to show the original purchase receipts and also depreciation schedules. Be sure to keep these papers for at least four years after the end of the allowable life for each piece of equipment.

*Things get more complicated if you decide to sell or trade-in a piece of equipment before its allowable life has ended. Again, it is essential to keep records. If a piece of equipment is sold, a record of the date and amount you are paid must be kept. If traded-in, a receipt must show the trade-in amount.

*It is also possible to take a piece of equipment originally purchased for personal use and convert it to business use. Conversely, a piece of business equipment may be converted to personal use. The date of such conversions is critical. Such changes must be reflected in calculating your tax deductions.

*If you own your home, you may also depreciate part of the cost of the room in your house that you use for teaching. The amount you can depreciate depends upon whether the room is used *exclusively* for teaching or, if not, the percentage of time it is used for teaching. This would involve calculating the fraction of the purchase price of your home that is attributable to your teaching room, usually based on a square-foot-of-floor-space formula. This teaching room is classified as *non-residential real estate* and is to be depreciated over 39 years in accordance with an IRS schedule. In 1993, changes were made to this allowable life.

*When your home is sold, there are further complications involving the rule regarding deferment of taxable income resulting from the sale. This rule would *not apply* to the teaching room portion. Also, if you are over age 55, the teaching room does *not qualify* for a tax exclusion.

Among the items which might be depreciated are:

Major Equipment:	*Accessories:*
Amplifier/Speaker	Adjustable Bench
(for guitar or keyboard)	Cassette Recorder
Desk	Microphone
File Cabinet	Music Display Racks
Instruments	Phone Answering Machine
Sound Module	Tuning Device
Stereo System	

*Consult a qualified tax advisor for these circumstances.

CHAPTER 44

ELECTRONIC KEYBOARDS

TEACHER CONSULTANT — SUE PENNINGTON

This chapter will help answer these and other important questions about keyboards.

1. Why are electronic keyboards so popular?
2. How do sound and touch compare to the piano?
3. What do I need to know about teaching keyboards?
4. Can I teach without an electronic keyboard in my studio?
5. Do I need special methods and teaching materials?
6. What do I look for when buying a keyboard?

Why Are Electronic Keyboards So Popular?

When compared to the conventional piano (often called an "acoustic" piano) the electronic keyboard is less costly, smaller, portable, and capable of different voices. It may be used with earphones and never needs tuning. It has special appeal to apartment dwellers where sound level, privacy, space, and ease of moving may be concerns. Families on a limited budget may be able to afford a small electronic keyboard but not a piano or organ.

Here is an important opportunity for piano and organ teachers. Individuals and families who have purchased electronic keyboards are all potential students. It may be simply an instrument with miniature size keys and 2½ octaves that was purchased in a discount store or toy store. Even this can be used as a starter instrument for a small child (up to about age seven) for Primer Level work. The miniature keys offer the same advantage for a small hand as the miniature violin which is used in teaching young children. It is also an excellent and inexpensive way for teacher and parents to evaluate the child's musical talents and interest — much better than any aptitude test. When beginning Level One, however, a keyboard with *full-size keys* (same as regular piano keys) and *at least four octaves* is necessary.

Older children and adults will need full size keys from the start. A four-octave keyboard will permit work through Level One. Five octaves are needed for Level Two through Level Four and will suffice for most of Level Five. Beyond this, a full size piano or electronic piano would be advisable.

To a serious musician, the refinement of touch-sensitivity has been the most significant development in keyboards. Although electronic, it enables the player to control the sound by touch, similar to the action of a piano. The heavier the touch, the louder the sound. Sophisticated keyboards are also *velocity-sensitive;* the speed with which the key is depressed produces slight changes in timbre. Just like the touch of different pianos, the touch-sensitivity of electronic keyboards varies among models and manufacturers.

There are currently three general types of electronic instruments with a keyboard.

1. ELECTRONIC KEYBOARD

This is the most common keyboard and is available with a wide variety of features and accessories. It is most likely to be the one a student would have at home.

Main Characteristics:
    Four or Five Octaves
    Easily Portable (10 to 20 pounds)
    Fits Tabletop or Floor Stand
    Built-in Speakers
    Many Different Voices (like organ stops)
    Never Needs Tuning
    Automatic Rhythm Background
    Automatic Chord Accompaniment
    Jack for Headphones
    Battery Operation

Common Optional Features:
    Chorus and Vibrato Controls
    Transposing Device
    Sustain Pedal (damper pedal)
    Expression Pedal (like swell pedal)
    May be Fine Tuned (for use with other instruments)
    Touch Sensitivity
    MIDI Capable (see page 185)
    Built-in Recording Device (sequencer, see page 185)

2. ELECTRONIC PIANO (or Digital Piano)

This keyboard is heavier (20 to 90 pounds) because of the weighted action used for the touch-sensitive keyboard. It is sometimes called a "digital piano" because of the digital electronics used to produce the sound.

Main Characteristics:
> 61, 76 or 88 Keys
> Touch-Sensitive Keyboard
> Sustain Pedal (damper pedal)
> Built-in Speakers
> Jack for Headphones
> Never Needs Tuning

Common Optional Features:
> Five to Seven Different Voices
> Soft Pedal
> Transposing Device
> Built-in Metronome
> Chorus and Vibrato Controls
> Built-in Recording Device (sequencer, see page 185)
> May be Fine-Tuned (for use with other instruments)
> MIDI Capable (see page 185)

3. SYNTHESIZER

This is used primarily by professional performers and is not suitable for teaching except for experienced players; certainly not for beginners. Like a personal computer, operating a synthesizer requires some technical understanding and patient experimenting to become proficient. Keyboards range from four octaves to a full 88 keys. The player has complete control of various sound generating elements which may be combined and blended in an almost infinte variety. Sounds range from those imitating conventional instruments to all kinds of "electronic" sounds and special effects. Prices go up into thousands of dollars.

Synthesizers are widely used in music composed for TV and movies. Many colleges and universities have developed programs using synthesizers for experimentation, performance, and serious composition.

Does An Electronic Keyboard Sound Like a Piano?

This depends upon the sophistication and quality of the instrument and also the discrimination of the listener. Although an untrained ear can be rather easily deceived, an experienced pianist will usually find electronic keyboard sound to be pleasant but nonetheless synthetic. However, some expensive keyboards that have sampled sounds (see page 186) come amazingly close to the sound of a real piano.

How Does Electronic Touch-Sensitivity
Compare To a Piano?

Again, this is determined by the design and quality of the instrument, as well as the training of the player. To a person with minimal keyboard skills, the differences in touch will seem slight. A well-trained musician with a sensitive touch may prefer the conventional piano, but find various degrees of satisfaction in different electronic instruments.

Advantages of the Electronic Keyboard for Practice

Practicing on an electronic keyboard may actually be better than on an out-of-tune or neglected piano. Poorly regulated action, sticky keys, missing hammers, or broken strings are certainly discouraging and an impediment to good progress. Most keyboards have a volume control and a headphone jack so that practice need not disturb others in the household. The whole keyboard may be carried to another room for practice free from distractions. Where there are two students in the same family, an electronic keyboard offers an inexpensive second instrument so that both pupils can practice at the same time.

What Do I Need To Know About Teaching Keyboards?

Teaching electronic keyboard or electronic piano is surprisingly close to teaching piano or organ. Your musicianship, knowledge of music and the keyboard, and your experience in teaching piano or organ are your most important qualifications.

IF YOU KNOW ONLY THE PIANO you will be able to easily teach the elements of keyboard musicianship. The student can learn note reading, rhythms, proper fingering, some technic, and good hand position while practicing on any electronic keyboard or electronic piano. If you accept a student with an electronic instrument, find out the make and model. Try to visit a dealer who has the same keyboard on display. Take time to play the instrument and ask a salesperson to show you how it works. If possible, get a brochure which pictures the keyboard and describes the features. This costs nothing and enables you to become acquainted with the type of instrument your student has at home.

If the student's instrument is easily portable, ask that it be brought along to the lesson. This is the best way to help the pupil progress efficiently. If transporting the instrument is a chore or hardship, perhaps it could be brought once or twice each month. If it cannot be brought at all, ask the student to bring the instruction manual for the keyboard to each lesson. You may want to keep the manual for a week or so to study it without taking lesson time.

The music rack for most keyboards is not designed for heavy books. If this is a problem, place a separate music stand (one which rests on the foor) behind the keyboard.

As a pianist, you will encounter some unfamiliar controls on an electronic keyboard. Although the number and variety of buttons varies from one instrument to another, they are grouped into three sections:

1. **Automatic Rhythm Background** is like a "drum machine" which repeats a 1 or 2-measure rhythm pattern over and over. The speed is adjustable, like a metronome, and a you may choose a pattern suitable to the style of music. Typical choices include country, waltz, march, slow rock, etc.

   The student should be thoroughly familiar with the notes and rhythm of a piece before adding a rhythm background. The speed control should be set quite slowly at first. Use of automatic rhythms may be helpful in maintaining a steady beat and providing ensemble experience.

2. **Automatic Chord Accompaniment** produces a repeating 1 or 2-measure arpeggio or broken chord pattern. It is linked to the style and speed of the rhythm background. When this feature is turned on, the keyboard is "split" into two sections. The upper section is used for melody. The lower section is used for determining the chord. One way is to hold down the notes of a 3 or 4-note chord. The keyboard will automatically

produce a broken chord accompaniment and repeat it over and over until you change to a different chord. Some keyboards allow you to determine the root of the chord by pressing just one key. There is usually a way to produce major, minor, and seventh chords as explained in the keyboard manual.

3. Different Voices are like organ stops. Typical choices are strings, brass, piano, clarinet, guitar, etc.

You'll probably enjoy taking time to learn the operation of these features — perhaps even taking a few lessons from a dealer. You may be surprised at how easy it can be. At first, you may want to limit the scope of your teaching until you feel more comfortable with the new mechanisms. If necessary, the student could go to a dealer who could help with the automatic rhythms, automatic chords, registration, etc.

Teaching of touch training and dynamics will depend upon whether or not the student's keyboard is touch-sensitive. If not, assume that the keyboard will have a touch similar to an electronic organ — needing careful control to achieve a legato. One very helpful accessory is an expression pedal, which operates like the swell pedal of an organ, controlling the volume of sound. Dynamics can be taught by the use of the expression pedal, even if the keyboard is not touch-sensitive. The student should be encouraged to buy this expression pedal, if available.

If the student's instrument is an *electronic piano* or *digital piano* you will be able to continue teaching to a higher level, depending on the number of octaves on the keyboard. The more advanced and subtle aspects of keyboard touch and musicianship, however, will need an acoustic piano.

Some electronic pianos offer no variety of voicing. For others, the choice is usually limited to about five voices such as Piano 1, Piano 2, Electronic Piano, Vibraphone, and Harpsichord. It is quite easy to let the student experiment with different voices for different pieces. For example, a vibraphone voice could be used for a piece in a romantic mood. A harpsichord voice could be used for Bach or Mozart. After more experience, the student can be shown how to change voices at different sections of the same piece, much as an organist would make changes of registration.

IF YOU ALSO KNOW ELECTRONIC ORGAN, either
spinet or console, you will find the automatic rhythms and
chord accompaniment devices are basically the same on
electronic keyboards. Because of different models and manufacturers, names of controls and their configuration will
vary. The same ideas for registration at the organ can be
used at the electronic keyboard. If the keyboard has an
expression pedal it can be taught the same way as the swell
pedal of an organ. Therefore, with organ training, you can
easily teach a student with an electronic keyboard.

SYNTHESIZER TEACHING. Unless you own a keyboard
synthesizer yourself and are proficient in its operation, you
should teach only keyboard basics to a student with a home
synthesizer. Be sure this is understood from the start. You
can provide a sound background in note reading, keyboard
technic, and theory. For a while the student may be satisfied
with experimenting at home on operating the synthesizer. Eventually, however, such students will have to be trans-
ferred to another teacher who can help with understanding
and using the synthesizer controls.

Can I Teach Without A Keyboard In My Studio?
Yes, but with some limitations. It will be easier if you have
both a piano and organ in your studio. A student with an
electronic *piano* as the home instrument should be taught
using your studio piano. If the student's electronic keyboard
is touch-sensitive, also use your studio piano. If not, the
pupil should use the organ during lesson time because of the
similarity in touch and controls. You may ask the student to
bring his home keyboard to each lessson, if possible.

Lessons are more productive if you have your own
keyboard in the studio. A low cost compromise is a small
4-octave keyboard with full-size keys ($150 or less at many
discount stores). Music dealers usually do not carry these
inexpensive keyboards.

Do I Need Special Methods and Teaching Materials?
For teaching keyboard basics, regardless of the home keyboard, you can use the same teaching curriculum that you use
for piano. The Schaum *Four Book Plan* involving method,
theory, technic, and reading materials is recommended (see
chapter 16). The level of advancement will depend upon the
number of octaves in the student's keyboard.

What Do I Look For When Buying a Keyboard?

It is best to try several different models and brands. Tone quality and touch are the most important factors. Desirability of features, ease of use, availability of repair service, reliability and expertise of the dealer should also be considered. If possible, talk with colleagues about their experiences.

As a teacher, you will probably be able to get a discount from the dealer. However, remember that a knowledgable dealer who can help you with the operation and answer your questions, perhaps simply by phone, is well worth a few extra dollars in the purchase price. Your studio keyboard should have the following as a minimum:

> Full Size Keys (same as an acoustic piano)
> Touch-Sensitive Keys
> At least Five Octaves (61 keys)
> MIDI-in and MIDI-out Receptacles (see page 185)

A student keyboard should be equipped the same, but could get along with only *four octaves* (49 keys).

Some students may have purchased a keyboard before coming to you for lessons. Their keyboard may not have all of the features recommended here. However, if it has *full size keys*, it is possible to use it for beginning lessons. Parents should be told that advancement will be limited by the capability of the keyboard and that trade-up to a better instrument will eventually be necessary, perhaps just after a few months of study.

The differences between electronic keyboards and electronic pianos are becoming less distinct as manufacturers cross over some features of one onto the other. As technology develops and competitive marketing continues, new features are continually evolving. It's a good idea to visit a keyboard dealer and see what's new at least once a year.

Some manufacturers now distinguish between an electronic piano and a digital piano, the latter being considered superior. A digital piano has entirely sampled sound and a better quality touch-sensitive action with weighted keys, making it closer to an acoustic piano.

What Is a Sequencer?

A sequencer is a digital recorder built into many keyboards. The technology is similar to that used for compact disks. It enables you to record as the keyboard is played. A sequencer has two main variables: 1) the number of tracks or voices 2) the length of time that can be recorded. Many inexpensive discount store keyboards have a simple, one track sequencer that can record a single note melody (with no accompaniment or harmony) about eight measures in length. A keyboard with a four track sequencer further expands this capability.

The length of recording depends on the size of the electronic memory built into the keyboard. Like a computer, the memory that stores the recorded music must have constant power – either from a battery or a wall receptacle. Remember, once the power is disconnected or the batteries removed, the recording is lost. A recording can be stored permanently on a diskette drive, like a computer. Some keyboards allow the digital recordings to be stored on a standard cassette recorder (but they can be played back only through the keyboard). Top of the line keyboards often have a built-in diskette drive to make and store quite lengthy recordings. Unfortunately, the diskette formats from different manufactures are not always interchangeable.

Most electronic *pianos* have a built-in sequencer that is easy to use – you simply record as you play. Electronic *keyboards*, however, usually record only one track at a time, layering one track on top of another to produce the full recording. This is rather tricky and time-consuming.

What Is MIDI?

MIDI is an acronym for "Musical Instrument Digital Interface." For a rather small extra cost, MIDI allows a keyboard to be connected to a computer, to another keyboard, or to be enhanced by accessories such as a diskette recorder, drum machine, rhythm/chord device or sound module. A *sound module* adds dozens of different sounds (like organ stops).

Difference between Sampled and Synthesized Sound.

The sound produced in electronic keyboards and pianos is either synthesized or sampled. The electronic building and blending of many sound elements needed to produce a musical timbre is called *synthesized sound.* In a synthesizer, the performer is able to adjust these sound elements to imitate conventional instruments or to produce custom sounds. In most electronic *keyboards* the sounds are synthesized but not adjustable. Some more expensive keyboards will allow a limited adjustment of a few sound elements.

A sampled sound is a digital recording of a real instrument and is, therefore, significantly more realistic than synthesized sound. Sampled sounds are found on most electronic pianos and in sound modules. More expensive units have more sophisticated samples. For example, in sampling a piano, each key may be struck at different dynamics and with different velocity. This may mean as many as six different samples for each pitch. A less expensive unit will have fewer samples for each pitch. Similar sampled sounds are available for virtually all band and orchestra instruments.

What Is a Sampler?

Some keyboards contain a "sampler" which enables you to digitally record *any sound,* such as a dog's bark or door slam and reproduce it on the keyboard at different pitches. This is done with a built-in microphone.

A more elaborate sampler is also sold as a separate device, sometimes with its own mini-keyboard, and may contain 100 or more pre-sampled sounds of traditional instruments as well as *non-musical* sounds such as breaking glass, ocean waves, or a lion's roar. It can be connected via MIDI to a larger keyboard and used for special effects.

What Is a "Split" Keyboard?

A "split" divides a single keyboard into two or more sections. For example, a 5-octave keyboard might be split so the top three octaves are used for melody notes and the bottom two octaves for automatic chord accompaniment. The use varies with the make and model of keyboard. It is also common to use the split for two different voices (functioning like the upper and lower manuals of an organ). Some instruments allow the split point to be moved up or down, varying the number of keys in each section.

CHAPTER 45

COMPUTER POSSIBILITIES

Computers have become quite common in music studios and in students' homes. This chapter will explain the current uses for computers in music teaching. Some of the information is very basic and intended for those who have limited computer experience. The chapter is divided into these sections:

A. Computers Can Be a Big Help

B. Planning a Computer Setup for Your Studio

C. Selecting and Using Software

D. Bookkeeping and Taxes

E. Graphics Programs

F. Music Notation

G. Musical Teaching Aids

H. CD Player in the Computer

A. COMPUTERS CAN BE a BIG HELP

Computers now offer many possibilities to help the private music teacher. There are software programs to help organize your studio, keep financial records and help prepare your tax returns. Word processing software helps create more professional looking printed forms including advertising, announcements, studio policies, information letters, correspondence, invitations and recital programs. Other software helps make customized greeting cards. A modem allows you to send and receive fax messages.

There is software to create your own printed music, with notes appearing on the computer screen as you play! Software can also make a digital recording of your playing on an electronic keyboard. Many software programs can be used as music tutorials or as remedial work for individual pupils. Some software offers specialized music training and music appreciation experiences.

Connection to the internet allows you access to information and catalogs of music dealers, music publishers and instrument manufacturers. It is also possible to order music and other products using the internet. The internet enables you to access library catalogs all over the country and numerous databases with all kinds of statistics and information. E-mail via the internet opens up world wide correspondence capability.

B. PLANNING a COMPUTER SETUP for YOUR STUDIO

The space needed and placement of the computer will depend on how you plan to use it. These basic questions will need to be answered to help in your planning:

Will computer use be limited to you and your household members? If so, the computer could be located almost anywhere in your home, including a bedroom or dining room. It is usually best to avoid the same room as your piano, TV or stereo.

Do you want to use the computer for composing, music notation or digital recording? If so, you will need an electronic keyboard or digital piano equipped with MIDI-in and MIDI-out receptacles. If you have a recent model electronic instrument, it probably has these receptacles. (See pages 178-79 and 185.)

Do you want your students to be able to use the computer for tutorial or remedial work? If so, it is desirable to have an electronic keyboard. Without the keyboard, many music software programs are limited in their effectiveness or cannot be used at all. The computer should be placed in a location where the student can work independently and not interfere with your teaching or the activities of other household members.

C. SELECTING and USING SOFTWARE

Before buying a software program, find out as much about it as you can. It is best if you can talk to someone who has already used the same kind of software. If you are a member of a teacher's association, you may be able to locate a colleague who has used the software you want to purchase. The music department at a nearby college or university may have a person who knows the software. If you can locate a person with this software, you might arrange to look at the software manual which provides step-by-step instructions. The publisher of the software may offer free literature describing details of the program. Sometimes, the internet may be a source of information.

Software magazines, usually available where magazines are sold, regularly review new programs and upgrades. Music software is often reviewed in music magazines. A public library may have back issues of magazines with the product review that you need.

Classes for learning specific software are offered by some computer dealers, colleges and adult education departments. These can be especially beneficial if they include individual computer work during the class. As with any class, it helps to take notes as you learn. You will get the most benefit if you can work at your home computer between classes.

Some popular software programs have instruction manuals published separately. "Wordperfect® for Dummies" is an example. These manuals are available at larger computer stores and at book stores.

D. BOOKKEEPING and TAXES

There are several inexpensive software packages that help with home finances, business finances and tax preparation. I use a program called Quicken®. It facilitates balancing a check book and helps organize your home finances.

QuickBooks® is a program for more complete accounting including payroll, general ledger, accounts receivable and accounts payable. Your dealer can furnish information on competitive programs.

E. GRAPHICS PROGRAMS

Many computers are bundled with basic software that can create typography, borders, decorative elements and simple drawings. These can be useful for advertising, announcements, invitations, recital programs, etc.

If you want to do more with graphics, look for software with libraries of borders, designs and fancy typography. Other software helps create posters and customized greeting cards.

F. MUSIC NOTATION

There are several software programs to create your own printed music. To function most efficiently, you should have an electronic keyboard equipped with MIDI-in and MIDI-out receptacles. Your computer may also need a sound card and special cables to connect your keyboard to it.

Music notation requires specialized software. Although some large computer dealers may have music notation software, you should also look at a music store which handles electronic keyboards and synthesizers. Very often someone on the store's staff can advise you and help you to obtain software.

G. MUSICAL TEACHING AIDS

There are a large number of software programs which can be used as music tutorials, for remedial work, supplementary note reading, specialized music training (such as theory or harmony) and for music appreciation. Catalogs of music software are sometimes free; others are available for a small charge, usually refundable if you place an order.

One source with an excellent catalog is:

Advanced Technologies
 a division of the Woodwind & the Brasswind
19800 State Line Road
South Bend, Indiana 46637
1-800-348-5003

You may also want to investigate a catalog called the Music Technology Guide from:

Lentine's Music
844 N. Main Street
Akron, Ohio 44310
1-800-822-6752

Warner Bros. Publications has a music software division called:

Electronic Courseware Systems
Warner Bros. Publications
15800 N.W. 48th Avenue
Miami, Florida 33014

H. CD PLAYER in the COMPUTER

A computer's CD-ROM drive has several uses. One is for loading software onto your computer. The CD-ROM may be required to access large files such as an encyclopedia or to operate some computer games. Most CD-ROM drives can also play music CD recordings, but with several advantages.

With your computer, you can access *any portion* of the music on the CD. This is useful if you want a student to hear a short excerpt in the middle of a movement that would not be accessible on an ordinary CD player.

When playing music CD's, it may be necessary for your computer to have a sound card and a separate amplifier and stereo speakers. In some cases, you can connect your computer to play through your home stereo.

CHAPTER 46

TEACHING PROGRAMS
for EACH LEVEL

PRIMER LEVEL TEACHING PROGRAM

At a BEGINNER'S FIRST LESSON

Assign one Method Book and one Theory Book.

METHOD Books:

For Age 4-5-6 .... See Chapter 34, "Ages 4-5-6"

For Age 7 to 10 .... Making Music at the Piano, Primer Level

For Age 11 to Adult .... Piano for Adults, Beginner Level

THEORY Books:

For Age 4-5-6 .... Keyboard Alphabet Workbook

For Age 7 to 10 .... Theory Workbook, Primer Level

For Age 11 to Adult .... Keynote Speller, Primer Level

Optional added Theory for Age 7 to Adult:

.... Rhythm Workbook, Primer Level

AFTER 4 to 5 LESSONS

Assign a Technic Book.

For Age 7 to Adult .... Fingerpower, Primer Level

AFTER an ADDITIONAL 2 to 3 LESSONS

Select one Repertoire book from the list on the next page.

Also select one piece of Sheet Music every 4 to 6 weeks.

(See list of solos on next page.)

Primer Level Repertoire Albums

Christmas:
  Christmas Favorites
  Christmas Primer
Classics:
  Great Ballets
  Great Composers
  Great Symphonies
Folk Music:
  Folk Song Primer
  §*Folk Songs and Dances*

Music for Fun:
  §*Festival of Solos*
  Patriotic Primer
  §*Piano Play Time, Primer*
  Repertoire Highlights,
    Primer Level
Sacred:
  Hymn Primer
  §*Sunday School Hymns*

Primer Level Sheet Music Solos

* = Big Notes   • = Original Form   ✋ = 5 Finger Position

*• At the Playground ✋ .... *John G. Revezoulis* §
*• Bike Hike ✋ .... *John W. Schaum* §
*• Bird Chorus ✋ .... *Alice McCullen* §
*• Bubble Gum ✋ (staccato) .... *Alice McCullen* §
  Christmas Tree Medley ✋ .. *Traditional / Arr. Jeff Schaum* ‡
*• Copy Cat .... *Lois Rehder Holmes* §
*• Every Witch Way ✋ .... *John G. Revezoulis* §
*• Happy Song ✋ .... *Lavoy Miller Leach* §
*• Jalopy Ride at the Fair ✋ .... *Wesley Schaum* §
*• Lollipop Waltz ✋ .... *John W. Schaum* §
*• Penguins at Play ✋ (left hand melody) .... *Julia Heim*
*• Playful Poodle ✋ .... *Margarite E. Schmidt* §
*• Puppy Love ✋ .... *Susan Sprengeler* §
* Scrambled Eggs ✋ .... *Margarite E. Schmidt*
*• Skating Along (left hand melody) .... *Margarite E. Schmidt*
*• Space Walk .... *Wesley Schaum*
*• Tomahawk Dance ✋ (minor key) .... *Cora Sadler Payne*
*• Whistling Along (optional duet accomp.) .... *Alfred Cahn*

§ = intended primarily for children
‡ = suitable for Christmas

LEVEL ONE TEACHING PROGRAM

Schaum's Four Book Curriculum

Assign one book in each category.

1. METHOD   **3. TECHNIC**

2. THEORY   **4. REPERTOIRE**

Level One books are usually assigned upon successful completion of the equivalent book at Primer Level. However, if the pupil is not near the end of the Primer Level method book, consideration should be given to assigning extra Primer Level supplements until the Primer method book is completed.

METHOD Books:

For Age 7 to 10 .... Making Music at the Piano, Level 1

For Age 11 to Adult .... Piano for Adults, Level 1

THEORY Books:

Keynote Speller, Level 1

Theory Workbook, Level 1

Sight Reading Workbook, Level 1

Rhythm Workbook, Level 1 (optional)

TECHNIC Books:

Fingerpower, Level 1

REPERTOIRE Books:

Repertoire Highlights, Level 1

Christmas:

  Christmas Solos, Level 1

  Easy Christmas Solos

Classics:

  Easy Master Themes, Level 1

  Great Ballets

  Great Composers

  Great Symphonies

Folk Music:

  Folk and Country Songs

Music for Fun:

  §*Dinosaur Ditties*

  §*Little Animal Tunes*

  Patriotic Primer

  §*Piano Play Time, Level 1*

  Sight Reading Solos

Sacred:

  Hymns of Hope and Joy

Level One Sheet Music Solos

* = Big Notes   • = Original Form   ✋ = 5 Finger Position   ✓ = Chord Symbols

*• Ancient Pagoda ....*David Biel*

*• Bubble Blues .... *Ladonna J. Weston*

*• Busy Woodpecker ✋ (staccato) ....*Alfred Cahn* §

 • Buzzy and Wuzzy (two kittens) ....*Guy Maier* §

*• Charm Bracelet ....*Alfred Cahn* §

*• Cheerleader...*Edward J. Plank* §

*• Dinosaur Land ....*Wesley Schaum* §

 • Fanfare ....*Stanford King*

✓ Hallelujah Chorus (easy edition) .... *Handel* ‡

* In the Hall of the Mountain King .... *Grieg*

* It Came Upon the Midnight Clear ....*Willis* ‡

 • Jolly Leprechaun ....*John G. Revezoulis* §

*• Kangaroo Hop .... *Mary Ann Polk* §

✓ Little Drummer Boy ....*Arr. Schaum* ‡

 • Opus One...*Alfred Cahn*

*• Perky Turkey .... *Ladonna J. Weston* §

*• Pony Ride ✋ .... *Dolores McCreary* §

✓ School Days ....*Gus Edwards*

 • Slumber Party.. *Molly Stecker* §

* Song of Joy ("Ode to Joy" from 9th Symph.) ....*Beethoven*

*• Spook House (left hand melody) ....*Wesley Schaum* §

* Spring, Sweet Spring...*Paul Lincke*

*• Spunky Spooks (both hands in bass clef) .. *Ladonna J. Weston* §

 Twelve Days of Christmas (all 12 verses) .... *Traditional* ‡

* What Child Is This? ("Greensleeves") .... *Old English Air* ‡

 William Tell March .... *Rossini*

*• Windshield Wiper Rock ....*Katheryn McCall Noblitt*

Piano Duet (1 piano, 4 hands)
 Parade of the Toy Soldiers ....*Leon Jessel* ‡

§ = intended primarily for children

‡ = suitable for Christmas

LEVEL TWO
TEACHING PROGRAM
Schaum's Four Book Curriculum

Assign one book in each category.

1. METHOD	3. TECHNIC
2. THEORY	4. REPERTOIRE

METHOD Books:

For Age 7 to 10 .... Making Music at the Piano, Level 2
For Age 11 to Adult .... Piano for Adults, Level 2
Chords and Improvising .... Easy Keyboard Harmony, Book 1

THEORY Books:

Theory Workbook, Level 2
Sight Reading Workbook, Level 2
Rhythm Workbook, Level 2 (optional)
Scale Speller (optional)

TECHNIC Books:

Fingerpower, Level 2
Czerny in All Keys, Book 1

REPERTOIRE Books:

Repertoire Highlights, Level 2

Christmas:
  Christmas Festival
  Christmas Solos, Level 2
Classics:
  Classic Themes, Book 1
  Easy Master Themes, Level 2

Folk Music:
  Stephen Foster Favorites
Music for Fun:
  Easy Boogie, Book 1
  §*Piano Play Time, Level 2*
  §*Sports and Games*

Level Two Sheet Music Solos

* = Big Notes   • = Original Form   ✓ = Chord Symbols

America the Beautiful .... *Samuel A. Ward*
• Circus Ponies .... *Lavoy Miller Leach*
*• Cool School .... *Wesley Schaum*
• Dominoes .... *Alfred Cahn*
• Dream Catcher .... *Lois Rehder Holmes*
• Dude .... *Ladonna J. Weston*
*✓ Entertainer (easy edition) .... *Scott Joplin*
*• Fawn's Lullaby .... *Carol Foster Masson*
*• Galloping Ghosts (minor key) .... *Weston / Schaum* §
*✓ How Great Thou Art .... *Swedish Folk Melody*
• Hurry, Little Pizza Car .... *Lois Rehder Holmes* §
• In a Far Off Time and Place .... *John G. Revezoulis*
*✓ It's Beginning to Look Like Christmas .... *M. Willson* ǂ
Mozart's Romance (from "A Little Night Music") .... *Mozart*
Pachelbel's Canon (easy edition) .... *Pachelbel*
Parade of the Toy Soldiers .... *Leon Jessel* ǂ
• Peaceful Interlude .... *Lois Rehder Holmes*
* Pogo Stick Chop (based on "Chop Sticks") ...... *Wesley Schaum* §
*• Roller Blades .... *Wesley Schaum*
• Scottish Sketch .... *Lois Rehder Holmes*
✓ Star Wars (Main Title) .... *John Williams*
• Sunset Serenade .... *Frank Levin*
✓ Take Me Out to the Ball Game .... *Albert von Tilzer*
Thanksgiving Scene .... *Medley of 4 Hymns*
• Water Slide .... *Cora Sadler Payne* §

Piano Duet (1 piano, 4 hands)
Hark the Herald Angels Sing .... *Mendelssohn* ǂ

§ = intended primarily for children
ǂ = suitable for Christmas

LEVEL THREE
TEACHING PROGRAM
Schaum's Four Book Curriculum

Assign one book in each category.

1. METHOD	**3. TECHNIC**
2. THEORY	**4. REPERTOIRE**

METHOD Books:

For Age 7 to 10 .... Making Music at the Piano, Level 3
For Age 11 to Adult .... Piano for Adults, Level 3
Chords and Improvising .... Easy Keyboard Harmony, Book 2

THEORY Books:

Theory Workbook, Level 3
Sight Reading Workbook, Level 3
Syncopation Workbook
Rhythm Workbook, Level 3 (optional)
Arpeggio Speller

TECHNIC Books:

Fingerpower, Level 3
Around the World in All Keys (scales, cadences & pieces)
Czerny in All Keys, Book 2

REPERTOIRE Books:

Repertoire Highlights, Level 3

Christmas:
  Christmas Classics
  Christmas Solos, Level 3

Classics:
  Classic Themes, Book 2
  Easy Master Themes, Level 3
  Hansel and Gretel
  Peter and the Wolf

Duets:
  Christmas Tunes for Two
  Tunes for Two, Book 2

Music for Fun:
  Easy Boogie, Book 2
  Easy Ragtime
  Parade of Marches
  §*Piano Play Time, Level 3*

Sacred:
  Hymns of Faith
  Jewish Folk & Holiday
    Songs

Level Three Sheet Music Solos

* = Big Notes   • = Original Form   ✓ = Chord Symbols

§ = intended primarily for children

LEVEL FOUR
TEACHING PROGRAM
Schaum's Four Book Curriculum

Assign one book in each category.

1. METHOD   3. TECHNIC
2. THEORY   4. REPERTOIRE

METHOD Books:

For Age 7 to 11 .... Making Music at the Piano, Level 4
For Age 11 to Adult .... Piano for Adults, Level 4
Chords and Improvising .... Easy Keyboard Harmony, Book 3

THEORY Books:

Theory Workbook, Level 4
Sight Reading Workbook, Level 4
Interval Speller (optional)

TECHNIC Books:

Fingerpower, Level 4

REPERTOIRE Books:

Repertoire Highlights, Level 4

Christmas:
Christmas Carols and Hymns
Christmas Songs and Tunes
Christmas Solos, Level 4
Music for Fun:
Rhythm & Blues, Book 3
Sacred:
Hymns and Gospel Songs

Classics:
Best of Bach
Best of Beethoven
Best of Mozart
Best of Schubert
Best of Tchaikowsky
Classic Themes, Book 3
Easy Master Themes, Level 4
Nutcracker Suite

Level Four Sheet Music Solos

• = Original Form   ✓ = Chord Symbols

‡ = suitable for Christmas

LEVEL FIVE
TEACHING PROGRAM
Schaum's Four Book Curriculum

Assign one book in each category.

1. METHOD   3. TECHNIC
2. THEORY   4. REPERTOIRE

METHOD Books:

For Age 11 to Adult .... Making Music at the Piano, Level 5
Chords and Improvising .... Easy Keyboard Harmony, Book 4

THEORY Books:

Chord Speller

TECHNIC Books:

Fingerpower, Level 5

REPERTOIRE Books:
Christmas:

Christmas Solos, Level 5

Classics:

American Sonatinas
Best of Chopin
Clementi Sonatinas
Handel's Messiah
Original Piano Classics
Peer Gynt Suites
Strauss Waltzes

Music for Fun:

Boogie is My Beat
Jazz Jamboree
Ragtime Rage, Book 1 (Scott Joplin)
Ragtime Rage, Book 2 (Scott Joplin)

Level Five Sheet Music Solos

• = Original Form   ✓ = Chord Symbols

✓ Alexander's Ragtime Band ....*Irving Berlin*

• Avalanche ....*Stephen Heller*

✓ Blue Danube ....*Johann Strauss, Jr.*

Circus Grand March ("Entry of the Gladiators") .... *Fucik*

• Contemplation (minor key) ....*Alfred Cahn*

• Curious Story ....*Stephen Heller*

Danse Macabre (minor key) .... *Saint-Saens*

Etude in E Major .... *Chopin*

Hallelujah Chorus .... *Handel* ‡

In the Hall of the Boogie King .... *Grieg / Schaum*

It Is Well With My Soul .... *Bliss / Cupp*

March from 6th Symphony (3rd Mvt.) .... *Tchaikowsky*

• Powerhouse ....*John W. Schaum*

• Rawhide...*Alfred Cahn*

• Rock Rhapsody ....*Stanford King*

• Romance ....*Frank Levin*

• Rustic Sonatina .... *William D. Armstrong*

Serenade...*Victor Herbert*

• Snazzy .... *Ladonna J. Weston*

Sweet Hour of Prayer ....*Bradbury / Cupp*

Piano Duet (1 piano, 4 hands)

Beethoven's 6th Symphony (2nd Mvt. Theme).......*Beethoven*

Rondo in A Major, Op. 107 ....*Schubert*

‡ = suitable for Christmas

LEVEL SIX
TEACHING PROGRAM
Schaum's Four Book Curriculum

Assign one book in each category.

1. METHOD **3. TECHNIC**

2. THEORY **4. REPERTOIRE**

METHOD Books:

For Age 11 to Adult .... Making Music at the Piano, Level 6
Chords and Improvising .... Easy Keyboard Harmony, Book 5

THEORY Books:

(continue) Chord Speller

TECHNIC Books:

Fingerpower, Level 6

REPERTOIRE Books:

Christmas:

Christmas Cameos
More Christmas Cameos
Still More Christmas Camoes

Classics:

(cont.) Clementi Sonatinas
Wedding Music

Duets:

Christmas Creations

Level Six Sheet Music Solos

• = Original Form   ‡ = suitable for Christmas

Ave Maria (cameo transcription) .... *Schubert* ‡
Canon .... *Pachelbel*
Carol of the Bells .... *Ukranian Bell Carol* ‡
Christmas Fantasy .... *Moore / Schaum* ‡
Clair de Lune .... *Debussy*
Greensleeves .... *Cameo Transcription* ‡
I Wonder as I Wander .... *Appalachian Carol* ‡
Jingle Bells Jubilee .... *Theme & Variations* ‡
Rise Up Shepherds and Follow .... *American Spiritual* ‡
• Solfeggietto .... *C.P.E. Bach*
Trumpet Fanfare .... *from "Masterpiece Theater"*

TEACHING AIDS • DICTIONARIES
FLASH CARDS

Items here are published by Schaum Publications, Inc.

DICTIONARIES

Chord Dictionary
Pocket size card; 12 different chords in 12 keys

Composer Dictionary
Over 680 composers, self-pronouncing: includes birth and
death dates, nationality, one-line biography

Dictionary of Musical Terms
1500 most-used words, large type, self-pronouncing;
special edition for all music students through high school

Music Dictionary
Pocket size card; 120 words

FLASH CARDS

Flash Cards: Set #1 (single note)
2 octaves above and below middle C; 34 cards

Flash Cards: Set #2 (melodic intervals)
White key 2nds, 3rds, 4th, 5ths, one octave above and
below middle C; 64 cards

TEACHING AIDS

Jumbo Staff Manuscript Book
24 detachable pages

Keyboard Notation Chart
Fits behind Black Keys; printed keyboard with
notes and letter names

Lesson Schedule Card
See page 35

Poster: "I Want You to Practice Every Day"
Uncle Sam with pointing finger; 9 x 12 inches; full color

INDEX

Most important pages are shown as bold numbers.

Personal Notes

Personal Notes

Personal Notes